Lighting FIRES

Randy Clark

CREATION
HOUSE
Orlando, FL

LIGHTING FIRES by Randy Clark
Published by Creation House
Strang Communications Company
600 Rinehart Road
Lake Mary, Florida 32746
Web site: http://www.creationhouse.com

Unless otherwise noted, all Scripture quotations are from the Holy
Bible, New International Version. Copyright © 1973, 1978, 1984,
International Bible Society. Used by permission.

Scripture quotations marked NKJV are from the New King James
Version of the Bible. Copyright © 1979, 1980, 1982 by Thomas
Nelson, Inc., publishers. Used by permission.

Clark, Randy 1952-
   Lighting fires / by Randy Clark.
      p. cm.
   ISBN: 0-88419-478-7 (pbk.)
   1. Clark, Randy, 1952– . 2. Vineyard Christian Fellowship-
-Clergy—Biography. 3. Evangelists—Biography.
4. Clark, Randy, 1952– .
I. Title.
BV3785.C553A3   1997   97-20075
269'.2'092—dc21   CIP
[B]

Printed in the United States of America
89012345 RPG 87654321

*I dedicate
this book to DeAnne, my wife,
best friend, and partner
in ministry.*

ACKNOWLEDGMENTS

I WANT TO FIRST thank Jesus for His grace and mercy toward me, His call on my life, His healing of my body, and saving my soul. I thank the Father for giving His Son on the cross. I thank the Holy Spirit for convicting me of sin, causing me to be born again, anointing me with His gifts, and empowering me with His baptism of fire.

Second, I wish to give thanks to DeAnne, my wife. She has been willing to live the lifestyle of a single parent one hundred seventy days per year while I have been away for renewel meetings somewhere in the world. I want to thank her for her service of love, for holding down the home front, and for doing the duties of both a mother and a father. Only God knows how much of the blessing on my life has been because of her prayers for me. Also, I want to thank her for all her help with the church we pastor. I believe it is true that here on earth she is often known as Randy's wife, but when we enter the pearly gates I will be known as DeAnne's husband. I thank her for being my best friend and partner in ministry. The Father certainly knows the sound of her voice more than mine.

I want to thank my children who have had to share their daddy with so many others. Thanks to Joshua, Johannah, Josiah, and Jeremiah. I have missed them very much while away from home. Thanks to Josh for going with me on some of the trips in the summer. He will never know how much joy it brings to my life when he travels with me. Thanks to Johannah for preparing the folders of pictures to take on the road. Thanks to Josiah and Jeremiah for bringing such excitement into my life and for being understanding when I have to leave.

I thank Dr. Bob and Debbie Martin for all their help with my book and booklets. Debbie is a great help with editing and grammar, and Bob has been very helpful with the theological parts of these works.

I want to thank Creation House and Alyse Lounsberry who contributed their professional expertise to this project.

I publicly offer my thanks to John Wimber who was used of God to first put hope in my heart that God had a plan for my life much greater than I had ever hoped. John believed in me and prayed for me. His seminars, conferences, and teaching created a much needed balance in my life as a Christian leader.

Thanks to John Arnott for inviting me to Toronto. He would not let me go home, but made me stay in Toronto those forty-two days in the winter of 1994. Thank you for making an unbelievable schedule fun. Thank you for your friendship and love. Thanks to John's wife, Carol, for the healing I received when she and Steve ministered to me.

Thanks to Jack Taylor who, before he ever heard of me, was a hero of mine. His writings were like gold to me in a land of poverty while I was attending college and seminary. Thanks for

The Hallelujah Factor. Thanks for the early morning breakfasts at the "Clock" in Melbourne. I also owe thanks to Barbara for sharing Jack with me.

Thanks to Tim Taylor, Jack's son, who did much research and hard work to make this manuscript possible.

Thanks to Mark Endres who, beginning in January 1995, became my assistant; in so doing he gave me back some time to spend with my family. I thank him for simply being who he is. I am thankful for his faithful service and love for me as a friend. Thanks for joinging the "fasts" so it would be easier for me. Thanks for going for it and hungering for the things of God with me. Thanks for your willingness to use the prophetic gift God has given you for His kingdom and His glory. A special thanks to Angela and Tommy for giving away their husband and daddy to serve others during all those special occasions when you wished he could be home.

Thanks to Gary Shelton who laid aside his own plans for ministry in order to become my worship leaders for the renewal meetings. Thank you for being the Lord's man of "steel fingers," sometimes playing your guitar and singing for up to five hours per night. Thank you for your friendship. Thanks to Anni, Lindsay, Kateland, and Caleb who gave you up as husband and father in order to travel with me. Thank you, Anni, for your prophetic gift, which you were willing to use in our meetings. Thank you for cying out in travail the night we saw the creative miracle which led to Ann being healed of Atypical Idiopathic Parkinson's Disease.

Thank you to all my associates on the staff of the Vineyard St. Louis. You have loved me through the difficult changes of the past three years. You are my best friends.

Thanks to the people of the St. Louis Vineyard. Your prayers early in this move literally broke the spirit of fear off of DeAnne. Your setting me apart into this ministry while continuing to be your pastor was a gift to the larger church body and to my family. We could not have done it without your support.

—RANDY CLARK

CONTENTS

PREFACE

IN NOVEMBER 1994 I heard from Happy Leman, a friend in Champaign, Illinois, that God had used a Vineyard pastor from St. Louis to bring powerful blessings to a group of leaders on a regional retreat. I had met this pastor years before. We were part of the same movement, yet we had not communicated for several years, except for some discussion on the telephone about evangelism. Hearing that God had used him immediately piqued my interest. My wife, Carol, and I had been in a long season of earnest seeking for more of the presence of the Lord. We had just returned from a life-changing excursion to Argentina where we witnessed a nation in revival. God had previously spoken to me, saying, "Give Me your mornings, and spend time with those who are moving in the power of the Spirit." We were attempting to do exactly that.

In the fall of 1993 we were given four very explicit prophetic words that revival was imminent. We returned from Argentina in November 1993 with great expectations that God was about to move in a very powerful way. We were delighted to hear that Randy Clark had been on a similar quest. When I spoke to Randy, I asked him to speak at our church. "Randy, how soon can you come to Toronto?" I asked excitedly.

The very earliest date was six weeks away. I shall never forget January 20, 1994. When Randy and his team began to minister to the people in my church, the Spirit of God fell powerfully upon us. It was explosive! The rest is history. Hundreds of thousands have been powerfully impacted by the Spirit of God. Well over a million have attended the nightly meetings that continue to this day.

Randy Clark is among the most honest and humble of men. He is also unassuming, so desirous of a close and intimate walk with the Lord, so prepared to give all that he is and has.

The meetings in Toronto were not hyped under his leadership nor fueled with charismatic enthusiasm. Randy shared his heart with us, and the Holy Spirit came in great power. We could not keep up with the testimonies because they were so numerous.

Marriages were wonderfully healed. Deep roots of rejection were pulled out. Physical healings occurred night after night as God gave His blessing. Most were "out" under the power of the Spirit for great lengths of time. Many had to be carried to their cars. I had never seen the likes of it in all my thirty-eight years of being a Christian.

The most thrilling thing about it was this: These were *my* people! This was *my* church! We were not among strangers or in a meeting where we knew only a few. I knew that my church would not "put this on." God had come powerfully among us! With all of our praying for revival, I never stopped to think what it might look like. This looked and sounded like a battlefield.

The dead and the wounded were everywhere, yet Randy was in his glory. He loved it.

I believe from Scripture that the Lord places a very high value on humility and vulnerability. I am sure this is the reason he chose a man like Randy Clark. He is well-trained for ministry and has had many years of pastoral and leadership experience. He can be very articulate, having a keen mind, yet he has managed to stay soft and pliable, teachable and humble, relating so well to ordinary folks. We owe him a tremendous debt of gratitude. We love him with all of our hearts. We count Randy and DeAnne Clark among our dearest friends.

God has subsequently entrusted to Randy an international ministry where he has been used of the Lord to bring great blessing to multiplied thousands of hungry hearts, lighting fires of revival across North America, Europe, and many nations. He is one of God's leading servants, being used powerfully as the refreshing for the church results in revival in the cities and nations of the world. Here, in his own words, is his story. Anticipating that there is much more of the Holy Spirit's presence for you and your ministry, it is my greatest pleasure to introduce this work to you.

—*John Arnott*
Toronto Airport Christian Fellowship
Toronto, Ontario, Canada

FOREWORD

I CROSSED THE TRAIL OF Randy Clark before I met him when I attended what was then the Toronto Airport Vineyard. Controversial manifestations notwithstanding, both my wife and I were met by God in a personal, powerful, and life-altering manner. Four months later I met Randy Clark when he spoke at a meeting in Melbourne, Florida, where I now reside. It was there that our personal friendship began.

At that time Brevard County, Florida, was experiencing a mighty visitation of God with continuing implications to this day. I am fully aware of the controversy that rages around the "Toronto Blessing" and its worldwide influence. I am in full agreement that no work of God among men remains, for long, without defect. I agree, however, with the prayer of John Wesley: "Lord, send revival without defects; but if that is impossible, send revival, defects and all!" My firm conviction is that if we can respond properly to the present moving of the Spirit, we may well be in the early stages of what will prove to be the greatest revival of history. This seems to be evident in worldwide proportions.

Like David, Randy Clark seems, on the human side, to be an unlikely candidate for worldwide influence. Yet the gracious providence of God has thrust him into that position. He is unpretentious, unassuming, and possesses a disarming innocence, which prompts my wife to dub him "God's little shepherd boy."

Though biographical in part, this book chronicles the story of the beginnings of this present move of God in a manner so as to present vital principles pertinent to any time frame and any set of events. To read it is to ride a roller coaster of emotions that finally lands at a higher level of hope for a mighty visitation that can change our nation and world.

My life and ministry have been greatly revised by what God is doing in the world today, and I have been deeply enriched by relationships with Randy Clark and John Arnott. Their lives make me desirous of greater-than-ever passion for the person of Christ and a greater-than-ever commitment to world missions.

With excitement and anticipation I commend this work, which is both a fetching story of a simple man with a "little ol' me" complex who is mightily used of God and a report of God's awesome, multi-faceted, worldwide plan to touch His people once again.

—*JACK TAYLOR, PRESIDENT*
DIMENSIONS MINISTRIES
INDIALANTIC, FLORIDA

INTRODUCTION

WHEN JOHN ARNOTT asked me to come speak at the Airport Vineyard church in Toronto, I was scared to death. I believed that God would use other men, but not me. Nevertheless, I agreed to speak.

Four days of meetings (starting on January 20, 1994), turned into a sovereign visitation of the Holy Spirit. Since that date an estimated 1.8 million pastors, leaders, and individuals from approximately two hundred nations have come to be touched by God. We have been blown away by what God has done.

To hear this story, one might think that this revival sprang up overnight. But the truth is that God was preparing the leadership many years in advance. My own life is a perfect example of how God did this.

I believe that for many years God has been preparing me for this particular time in my life and ministry. In 1984 the Lord showed John Wimber that I would one day be involved in some type of translocal ministry. But it took ten years for that ministry to take shape. I believe God had to place values and foundations within me first in order for that translocal ministry to come forth. Thus I experienced a long period of "hiddenness" while God worked within me, preparing me for what He is now using me to do for Him.

This book is not so much about my ministry as it is about God's process of *preparation* for ministry. It's about how God, in His sovereignty, can even overcome our failures and straighten out the mess we've made of our lives. It's about the rescuing aspect of God's grace and the restoring aspects of His love and mercy. It is also about how God works through hardships to train us in faith and perseverance. It's the story of how God overcame the various fears and inadequacies of my life to give me the desires of my heart. It's the story of the "thrill of victory and the agony of defeat." It's the story of God's fire and how He first worked *in* my life, then *through* my life. It's the story of moving from refiner's fire to refiner's fire, desperately praying always to be used by Him to light other fires—fires of evangelism. This is the story of how God found a common man whose only virtue was his openness to be used for God's purposes.

Submitting to God's process of preparation changes us. I believe that God chose me to be a part of this new global move not because I was a dynamic speaker, but because I was open and yielded to Him. When a pastor of one of St. Louis's large charismatic churches heard that God had been using me in Toronto for a real revival, his comment was memorable: "Yes, I know Randy Clark of St. Louis—but it couldn't be him! There must be *two* Randy Clarks of St. Louis, because this man you're speaking of *couldn't possibly be the one I know!*" When I heard his response to how God had been using me in ministry, I was instantly reminded of how God again and again has chosen the weak and foolish things of the world to confound the strong and the wise. That being said, I guess I am uniquely qualified to continue to do the job I'm doing for God!

God is awesome, and I am constantly amazed that He has chosen to work through me in the areas of revival and personal ministry in these last days. I'm a young man, relatively speaking—but I have seen many mighty manifestations of the Holy Spirit in the course of my years of ministry.

If I had to name one thing that triggered the move of God in my life, it would be difficult to do. I can simply say that ever since I was empowered by the Holy Spirit, I have had a great hunger to know God more intimately and to walk with Him more closely. I have seen God move powerfully and in unusual ways. I have, from the sidelines, watched God sweep through meetings and touch His people in ways I had never previously seen. And, in the process, He has changed me. He has opened up my thinking. He has removed barriers within me that were hindering the anointing. And He has absolutely convinced me, without a doubt, that He is sovereign, and His awesome power cannot be boxed, canned, or contained.

You see, I experienced many failures and personal setbacks before God began to sweep me along on this great new wave of global evangelism, with signs and wonders following. I felt that I had failed at just about everything.

Repeatedly, seasons of hardness came with little spiritual fruit to show for my efforts. I experienced discouragement and spiritual weariness. And yet God continually refreshed my vision for souls and revival. Such vision invariably filled me with a sense of unbelievable irony: How could the Lord ever use someone like me to impact lives in any way, much less on the great scale of global evangelism? But that's what God had dropped in my heart, and that's the work I am doing today.

Again and again we have heard, "God is doing a new thing!" I know I've said it many times. But before I could truly experience this fresh new move of God, He had to do some things inside me. Having just said, "God is doing a new thing," I still sat quietly in a meeting conducted by the evangelist Rodney

Howard-Browne . . . and resisted what God was doing in and through him. I resisted the manifestations of laughter and unbridled joy that seemed to be breaking out all around me . . . until the Lord dealt with me on a deeper level. I allowed Him to clear away the spiritual debris that kept me from receiving from this anointed man of God. And there were other obstacles the Lord had to remove—my disdain for the ministry of deliverance and my aversion to the prophetic gifts.

This wave of evangelism is touching and transforming everything in its wake—our attitudes, our thinking, our approach to ministry, even how we do it. It is large. It is great. And, like a wave or a mighty spiritual wind, it is sweeping the globe. If we let it, it will change us too.

It is awesome. It is powerful. I stand in reverent awe of what God is doing on earth today. In fact, I'm blown away!

—*RANDY CLARK*
ST. LOUIS, MISSOURI

ONE

PASSION

*And how can they preach unless they are sent? As it is written,
"How beautiful are the feet of those who bring good news!"*
—ROMANS 10:15

PASSION FOR CHRIST has been a part of my life since the very beginning. Ever since receiving Christ as a teenager, I have known such spiritual passion. I have also grieved as my passion seemed to wane and lessen during certain seasons of my life. Because passion for Jesus is such a necessary element to effective evangelism, I have learned to guard it. But to guard one's spiritual passion is something only the Holy Spirit can teach.

When we first come to Christ, there is such a surge of spiritual passion, it seems that we can hardly contain it. We want to preach to everyone . . . to everything . . . even to inanimate objects! We are brimming over with the love of God, and so

1

naturally we want to see everyone as enthusiastic about Jesus as we are. It's a wonderful thing to have that much passion for Christ.

Then we begin our Christian walk, and things happen to test us; we discover that our spiritual passion has lost some of its sizzle. So we begin to settle in spiritually and adjust to the mundane aspects of our life with Christ . . . that is, until something happens to light the fire of the Holy Spirit and make us more passionate than ever!

That's what the Holy Spirit did for me when He empowered me in 1989. I thought I had experienced the pinnacle of what God had for me . . . that things just couldn't get any more exciting. How was I to know that God had so much more and was just waiting for me to reach out and grab it? Once I did, He turned up the burners on my spiritual passion even higher, creating in me an intense hunger for Him that consumes me to this day.

Out of that hunger I have ministered to countless thousands about the power of the Holy Spirit and the signs and wonders I have seen Him perform—well, they continually blow me away. God is so awesome!

When I minister around the world and the Holy Spirit begins to move, many thousands "fall out" under the power of God—believers and skeptics alike. As I stand there on the platform, looking out at that great sea of humanity, I can hardly believe that God could use me even just a little.

If the truth be told, I am the one who is most surprised that God could ever use me. You see, I'm not "Mr. Perfect"—I haven't done everything right. I have stubbed my toe, stumbled, even fallen backward for almost a year. I made bad decisions, and I paid the consequences for over two decades. There are many reasons why I almost didn't make the cut into ministry. Yet God decided to use me—the grandson of an illiterate, praying grandmother . . . the kid from the poorest regions of the Midwest, from a town where no one had much hope of succeeding.

But in order to describe the way the Holy Spirit has turned up the burners of my passion for Christ and the incredible spiritual journey that has been the result, I find it necessary to go back to the very beginning. . . .

BACK TO MY ROOTS

I was eventually saved in the small church I had attended almost every Sunday of my life growing up in southern Illinois. I had attended church almost every Sunday of my life growing up. My upbringing was simple; we lived in one of the poorest counties in America. I was not expected to amount to much, and even the pastors who ministered in our church didn't have high-school educations. In their cheap, chain-store suits, they gave God their best. But they were certainly no theologians. The expectations were not that high—even for a young man from our community who aspired to become a minister.

Yet I cannot remember a time in my life when I did not believe in my heart that the happiest people I knew were dedicated Christians. I had discovered this by watching their lives when I was a very young boy. The most dedicated Christians were the ones who demonstrated outwardly the most joy, peace, and love. They were the ones with solid marriages and happy families, attributing their love for Christ as the only real secret to all that happiness.

Unfortunately, what I saw taking place among the people in our church was not as idyllic. By my twelfth birthday our Baptist church had split four times. I have never forgotten some of the horrible animosity exhibited during some of those internal "cat fights."

Once I remember asking my mom, "Why can't all the churches just work together?" That's how idealistic I was, and it bothered me that our church members couldn't even get along with each other, let alone with believers from the other churches in town.

There were ten to fifteen Baptist churches within a ten-mile radius of our church, each with about fifty members. While still very young, I recall thinking, *How much more could get done if everybody just worked together?*

I learned such simplicity of faith from my illiterate grandmother. A passionate worshiper, she deeply loved the Lord and spent many hours daily praying and singing to Him. Since she

3

couldn't read, she couldn't read the Bible. So she listened for several hours each day to the Word as it was preached over the radio. Because she devoted herself to Him, she knew the Lord very well. She immersed herself in His presence and lived her life accordingly.

My grandmother was a "shouter." Even though we were Baptists, she would walk down the aisle shouting praises to God. The first time I ever witnessed laughter in the Spirit was when my grandmother led a testimony service. The Spirit of God came upon her, and she began to laugh and could not stop laughing until the anointing lifted.

At age seven I had come under conviction of the Holy Spirit to give my life to Christ, but I had not yielded because I had wanted to keep my macho image intact. I knew that if I went forward to receive Christ, I would cry, and I didn't want to do that in public. So for nine years, Sunday after Sunday, I had held back.

Not wanting anyone to know how I felt inside, I would lie down on the pew while the pastor preached and put my arm over my face to shield my eyes in an effort to make those around me think I was asleep. But I wasn't asleep; I was crying and quietly praying . . . *Oh, God, please don't make me cry! Please! Maybe I'll give You my life next week!*

Next week became the next week, and so forth, until nine long years had passed. *After all,* I reasoned, *I'm really not such a bad kid. I don't smoke and cuss and drink. I don't lie and cheat.* Inside, however, I knew that good behavior was not enough to get me into heaven. I paid attention in church and knew from the sermons I had heard that Jesus loved me and wanted me to commit my entire life to Him. My biggest sin had become my unwillingness to dedicate my life to Christ.

But one day in 1960, as my mother left a home church meeting, the Holy Spirit suddenly came upon her, and she fell to the ground. Afterward she related that it was as if something "hit" her, and she began to feel as if she were spinning. She likened the experience to being "caught up in a tornado." After the spinning stopped, she said she drifted down into a beautiful place too lovely to describe. During an out-of-body experience where she was caught up to heaven, she saw herself lying on the ground as though dead. Then a man approached her who, although He resembled none of the pictures of Jesus she had ever seen, was, nevertheless, the Lord. She simply knew that as a fact. He did not speak but communicated with her by looking into her eyes, smiling, and transmitting the thought, *Everything is going to be all right.*

My dad and I were both unsaved at the time, and Dad was having difficulty going to church. This thought imparted to my mother from Jesus caused great peace to come upon her. After awhile, she said she knew it was time to go back, and her spirit floated peacefully back into her body; then she sat up, dazed. For several days afterward, she floated around the house like a sleepwalker, with a starry look in her eyes, telling us, "It's so beautiful! It's so peaceful! I don't want to stay here—I want to go back!" Often she'd go out to the car, get in, and drive away.

Dad thought she was going crazy. He would try to reason with her, saying, "We have three little children! You *can't* leave!"

But she would reply, "I don't want to stay here. I want to go back. It's so peaceful!"

She snapped out of it before long, but to this day each time she relates the story she gets teary-eyed and finds it difficult to speak. As a result of my mother's heavenly experience, it wasn't long before my dad was saved.

And then it was my turn. It came as I neared my sixteenth birthday.

HAPPY BIRTHDAY TO ME!

It was just a few days until my sixteenth birthday, and for some reason I had decided to go to church on Sunday night. I could still remember the sermon preached by Rev. Jack Haygood when I was seven years old. He preached about Lot's wife and how vital it is that we come to Christ and not look back. On that night so long ago, I had listened to the preaching and cried silently because I knew God wanted me to give Him my life. For the next nine years I had resisted the Holy Spirit.

As my sixteenth birthday approached, I found myself again in church, resistant as ever, listening to a powerful sermon that convicted me of my sins and my need for Christ to cleanse me of them. I was afraid, but I was under such a load of conviction that I found it more and more difficult to postpone my decision to receive Christ as Lord and Savior. I was deeply moved when my Uncle Reno, who has Down's syndrome and stutters when he speaks, rose to his feet in the midst of a crowd of about twenty and announced, "I wwwwant t-t-to ppppp-p-pray th-a-tttt R-r-r-rrrrrandy bb-b-b-beee s-s-ssssaved t-t-ttttonight." I melted immediately.

I had successfully resisted shaking hands with the pastor, who had asked, "Randy, don't you want to be saved?"

I had answered, "Yes, but not tonight."

I had survived looking my grandfather in the eye, who had said not one word. I had pushed aside the various comments that came from the leadership of the church. But Uncle Reno's remarks got to me and melted my heart.

Just then my Sunday school teacher put her hand on my shoulder and asked, "Honey, don't you know God loves you?"

That did it for me. I broke down and wept.

I ran to the altar, crying all the way, and dropped to my knees at the old mourner's bench. "God, please forgive me for my sins!" I begged as great sobs racked my body. I confessed every sin I could think of, and then I asked Jesus to take control of my life.

The church members crowded around me, praying loudly that I would "pray through" and be truly "born again."

Many years later, I learned that on this same night the Lord had told my praying grandmother that I would one day be called to preach the Word.

Thus, my sixteenth birthday became my most memorable; not only did I enter a new era of young adulthood, but I was also born again. What a great birthday present!

CONFUSED ABOUT HEALING

I had already had several encounters with the truth that God heals by the time my grandfather was diagnosed with prostate cancer. I had my first personal encounter with healing when my grandmother was supernaturally healed of a goiter on her neck that had become swollen and painful. One day she heard the voice of the Lord tell her to go to the bedroom and pray. She obeyed the inner prompting and told me later, "As I was praying, it felt as if a hot hand went down my throat." The goiter instantly vanished and did not return.

Next I was among a group of believers from our church who prayed for my Sunday school teacher, Emmogean Campbell, who had been diagnosed with cancer. She had a tumor the size of a foot basin.

A group of us gathered to pray for her; when she went into surgery, the surgeon discovered that the huge tumor had shrunk to the size of a grapefruit and was no longer attached to any of her organs. Even the surgeon attributed this change to the power of prayer.[1]

So from my earliest memories, it just seemed to make sense that God still operated in the miraculous realm much the same as He did when Jesus walked the earth.

When my grandfather was diagnosed with prostate cancer, I expected God to heal him. But when he died after an agonizing year battling the disease that had metastasized and gone into his bones, I was devastated. It had been very difficult for me to watch him suffer.

In spite of my own prayers for his healing . . . in spite of the fact that churches from all over the state had been praying for him . . . he died.

I reasoned that having a grandfather in heaven made heaven all the more precious to me. But the truth was that I was completely confused.

I did not know what to do with the fact that I had seen two people healed—yet my grandfather had not been healed in spite of the fervent prayers of many Christians. At the time it just didn't make sense to me that he *had not* been healed when my grandmother and my Sunday school teacher *had* been touched by God's supernatural healing power.

THE SLIPPERY SLOPE

Perhaps it was my confusion and spiritual disorientation over my grandfather's death that started me down the slippery slope toward a year of miserable backsliding. I changed churches and started attending the First General Baptist Church in nearby McLeansboro.

The pastor, Bill Duncan, had once been a traveling evangelist. But he was forced to come off the road after his vocal chords were damaged when he hemorrhaged from the strain of preaching.[2] Although he had become a pastor, he still preached with the same fire and fervor that had marked his evangelism ministry. I was greatly influenced by his concern for the lost and his evangelistic zeal. Under his direction I became a leader in the youth group. I was a normal high-school student who seemed to be doing everything right. On the outside it appeared that I had it all together; on the inside I had some questions that weren't being answered. Maybe I didn't even know how to verbalize them. I kept right on doing the only thing I knew how to do—keep up the appearance of having it all together.

I was dating a pretty girl named Doris who lived in a nearby town. Her brother, Larry Hunt, was a preacher. I so respected him that sometimes, instead of going on dates, Doris and I would go over to where Larry was preaching and listen to his sermons. He believed, as I did, in God's supernatural power. I was especially impressed that Larry didn't talk much about healing. Instead he anointed sick people with oil and prayed for them to be healed. And some of them were healed.

Before very long I realized that I had fallen in love with Doris and wanted to marry her when we were old enough. But her mother was against the relationship.

The family soon moved away, and again I was devastated emotionally. My devastation threw me into a state of spiritual disappointment and disillusionment; it would be years before my heart was healed. I would eventually marry on the rebound after I learned that Doris was engaged to marry someone else. Often during the next three years I would find myself wondering how different my life might have been . . . how much happier . . . and how much hurt might have been avoided . . . if only I had married Doris.

When I turned eighteen I stepped away from the Lord and lived as a hypocrite for eleven months. In church every Sunday morning and every Sunday night it seemed that nothing much had changed. I attended the youth group before every Sunday evening service. I was just as involved as ever and, on the outside, seemed to be "Mr. Model Christian." But I had fallen into sexual immorality and had developed the habit of smoking pot daily. One day I realized just how unhappy I had become. There I was, acting as if I were part of the youth group same as always, as if nothing at all had changed—and the minute I left church I was hanging out with my cousin George and his best friend, Joe Barker. They moved in the fast lane.

We were known as the "Three Musketeers."

THE THREE MUSKETEERS

Smoke pot and get stoned. That's all we did. We may have talked about doing something with our lives—but that's all it was . . . just talk. One afternoon we got stoned and drove over to Dickerson's Drive-In, the local hamburger shop, to check out the super cars. As we pulled in at Dickerson's, I turned up the volume on Steppenwolf's hot new rock song, "The Pusher." The famous lyrics that again and again took the Lord's name in vain went blasting out our car windows and all over the parking lot.

The next day Larry Hunt called my house while I was out and left a message with my mother. "Tell Randy I saw him at Dickerson's. Tell him he didn't seem like the old Randy I know." I knew exactly what he meant. I phoned Larry back, set up a meeting, and prayed with him to rededicate my life to Christ.

But my commitment didn't last long. The lure of the "Three Musketeers" was just too strong a pull. Pretty soon I was back running with George and Joe, doing drugs, and having sex with my girlfriend. But I was still miserable.

One Sunday I went to my youth leader, handed him my

drugs, and asked him to pray with me to rededicate my life.... again. This time I was serious. We went to the altar, and I asked the Lord to take me back. Afterward I immediately broke up with my girlfriend.

But I remained friends with George and Joe, even though this time I kept my commitment to the Lord and stayed away from taking drugs.

One day the "Three Musketeers," along with Joe's sister, were driving home from junior college. I was getting plenty of ribbing for my "getting religion." Joe had told me a few days earlier that he was Catholic, although I couldn't see any evidence of his religious convictions since he continued to get drunk and stoned daily. "When I turn thirty, I'll get serious and become a good Catholic," he boasted. "But right now I want to live it up!"

Then George chimed in, "Clark, come on—admit it! You know that if we were in a wreck right now and you died, you'd go to hell!"

Joe said, "Yeah—that's right!"

But I insisted, "No, Joe—I wouldn't go to hell. But how about you?"

Five minutes later an oncoming car struck us and knocked us off the road and into a telephone pole and concrete culvert.

GOD'S WAKE-UP CALL

If ever I have experienced God's "wake-up call," that was it. The crash happened so fast . . . and, because I was knocked out instantly, I don't remember a lot of what happened. By all reports we flipped end-over-end three times, hit a telephone pole, and landed upside down in a ditch. Joe was thrown from the car and killed. George wasn't badly hurt; he was just knocked unconscious. Joe's sister was severely injured; her wire-rimmed glasses were driven up under the skin of her forehead, and her leg was badly broken. I was in shock and also badly injured. To this day I have no recollection of the events at the scene of the accident. I don't remember being pinned inside the vehicle or being taken out by the emergency crew that loaded us into the waiting ambulances. I don't remember saying over and over again, "Help me! Help me! I'm pinned in!"

But George remembers. He related to me that he had seen the passing car hit us and that he could hear me crying out to be rescued. Hearing about it, I was reminded of a childhood dream in which I went walking through the woods. In the dream a tree fell on my stomach, and I cried out, "Help me! Help me! I'm pinned down!" Then Jesus appeared and lifted the tree off me so that I was able to get up and walk.

Sixty stitches later, the lacerations in my face had slowly begun to heal. Some of my facial bones had been crushed. Three areas the size of quarters were crushed along my hairline, just above the forehead. The forehead itself had multiple fractures. A piece of bone the size of a dime was missing over my left eye. My left cheekbone was smashed.

The discs in the middle of my spine were compressed by 20 percent, resulting in nerve damage. I had several broken ribs, and my digestive tract was paralyzed. The doctors told my parents that I would be in the hospital anywhere from seven to eleven weeks, and they warned that it would be very dangerous to move me. To turn me, three nurses would pretend I was a log and roll me over.

I was in a state of delirium most of the time. A male nurse told me later that hour after hour in my medicated haze I would ramble on about God and also about drugs.

When I finally came to my senses four days later, bits of that final conversation with the "Three Musketeers" drifted in and out of my consciousness. Recalling that eerie conversation just minutes before the crash, I could still hear George's words ringing in my head: "Clark, come on—admit it! You know that if we were in a wreck right now and you died, you'd go to hell!"

I could hear Joe's reply: "Yeah—that's right!"

And I could hear my own: "No, Joe—I wouldn't go to hell. *But how about you?*"

When I was lucid enough to concentrate, Dad came into my room one day and asked me if I wanted a television set brought in. I told him *no*. I didn't want a TV—I wanted a Bible. This was unusual for me, considering that in spite of being raised in church, the only Scriptures I had read entirely on my own consisted of a few psalms. And I'm ashamed to admit it, but I had used my Bible plenty of times to hide the cigarette papers I had used to roll my marijuana joints. The accident shook me to the very core. Now I wanted to know for myself what was contained in the pages of the Bible.

Because of my injuries, I could not sit up to read. I couldn't even have a pillow. So the hospital staff gave me a pair of glasses fitted with reflective mirrors. With these I could lie in bed, place my Bible on my chest, and read the words as they were reflected in the small mirrors. Now I was reading because I wanted to know what God was speaking to me—personally. I fell in love all over again with Jesus, and I felt absolutely overwhelmed by the knowledge of His love for me.

I vividly remember praying, "Lord, You spared my life! I should be dead now, but You spared me. I give my life back to You. I'll do anything You want me to do, but please *don't call me to preach!*"

Firsthand Knowledge of Healing

While I knew that God could heal, I had never personally experienced a mighty manifestation of God's miracle-working power. Little did I know that I was about to experience the healing power of God for myself.

From the very beginning of my hospitalization, I was in pretty bad shape. Because of the exhaustive nature of my injuries, I was being given fifty milligrams of Demerol every three hours, with an extra dose at night. Even so, after two hours I would wake up in excruciating pain. I knew I needed a touch from God—I was growing weary of the pain and inactivity.

Many people came to pray for me, including my great-uncle Harry Neal, a Pentecostal preacher. Before too long I began to experience some manifestations that indicated I was being healed. Because my digestive system was still paralyzed, my doctors had wanted to move me from Mount Vernon Good

Samaritan Catholic Hospital to Barnes Hospital in St. Louis, Missouri. At midnight on the night before I was scheduled to be transferred, some young friends of mine went to the church to pray for me. They prayed until each had a strong sense of peace that I would be okay.

The next day some routine tests were performed prior to my transfer—tests that revealed that my digestive system was no longer paralyzed!

Later the same day, a doctor came to my room to set the jaw that had been broken in the crash. When he looked at my jaw, a curious expression began to creep across his face. "Put your teeth together," he ordered.

As I obeyed, he said, "Do it again!" I did it again.

"Do it again!"

I did. Finally, he said, "I don't understand it. I came in here to set your broken jaw—and it's already set!"

I began to wonder if God had healed me because He had heard me claim again and again that I was going to go to a revival meeting scheduled to take place in our town in just four weeks. But God wasn't through performing His miracles of healing yet.

The next day, all pain left my spine. I still felt stiff and weak, but the excruciating pain was completely gone. I had been told not to move or I might become paralyzed. But I knew God was doing something! As faith rose within me, I let down the bed's railing, swung both legs over the side, and stood up! I didn't realize that a person who had been bedridden for as long as I had been would inevitably become both dizzy and nauseous when standing for the first time. But neither of those symptoms came over me. My feet tingled; otherwise, I felt fine. It so alarmed a nurse who saw me as she stepped into my room that she yelled, "Get back in bed and don't do that again!"

But over the next few days I continued to test my strength, confirming my faith that I was, in fact, healed by God.

I told everyone who would listen that God had healed me—even the Catholic sister-nurse who came into my room one night to chastise me for sitting up for so many hours during the day.

"You've got to lie down!" she ordered. "You're jeopardizing your health; you could become paralyzed!"

That's when I dropped the bomb: "Sister, do you believe Jesus heals today?"

"Yes," she answered.

"That's good," I said, "because He just healed me. He has a purpose for my life and for my future, and He's not going to let me be paralyzed."

The staff hurriedly brought in a back brace that I wore—begrudgingly—as somewhat of a compromise when my mom was around, just so she wouldn't worry. But most of the time it lay on the bed as I read my Bible or walked the floor, praying. My recovery was going great—so well, in fact, that I went home after only twenty days instead of the seven to eleven weeks estimated by the doctors' original prognosis.

GOD HAD A PLAN . . .

The first Wednesday of November 1970 I gave my testimony in church at a youth service. The kids who heard me were ready to receive all God had for them. Four days later, at six o'clock on the night of the first Sunday of November, the power of God fell among the young people.

Everyone present that night came under strong conviction by the Holy Spirit. All of us went to each other, repenting and confessing the hurts we had caused. Forgiveness and much weeping took place. The presence of God was so sweet that the service carried over into the adult service at seven o'clock. Our pastor recognized the power and the presence of God and let the work of the Holy Spirit continue uninterrupted. The adults were just as affected as we were by what God was sovereignly doing.

As the deacons considered what had happened, they decided to ask the evangelist who was scheduled to come the following week if he could reschedule and come a week early. He agreed. When he arrived, a revival broke out that lasted six weeks. The place was packed every night. Almost everyone in the local high school came. At the end of the six weeks of services, there had been two hundred fifty professions of faith and eleven young men called into the ministry. One of those eleven young men was *me*. That became the first real move of God in which I had taken part. How was I to know that this was only the beginning?

Another cool thing happened to me in that time period: The Lord gave me a prayer language. It's what the Pentecostals refer to as "tongues." I didn't know what to call it, so I didn't call it anything. I just knew my prayer language was from God.

CALLED TO PREACH

When we were kids, my mother and grandmother cleaned the little Baptist church we attended. My kid brother, sister, and I would "play church" as they went about their cleaning duties. My sister, Vicky, would pretend to play the piano while my younger brother, Ricky, age seven, would play the part of the guy who got saved. I was always the preacher. I chose to be the preacher because, even at the ripe old age of nine, I wanted to be "successful," and my definition of success was to get somebody saved.

Shortly after I gave my life completely over to Jesus Christ, I began to get little sermon ideas whenever I read the Bible. I would share some of these with a younger preacher. Often he'd say, "Well, you ought to preach them!"

"I'm not called to preach!" I shot back.

Now here I was, called to preach. Or was I? Preaching was the one thing I had to be sure about. I had to know for certain that, out of my passion for Christ, I wasn't making the whole thing up.

When I look back with the glorious gift of 20/20 hindsight, I can see the hand of God and how He had been drawing me into the ministry even as a small child. My mom and grandma had seen the call of God on me. But it had taken a little while for me to see it. Finally I did.

Mom recalls how worried she was about me during those eleven months I was a backslider. She would confess her fears about my future to my grandma, who would comfort her by saying, "Don't you worry! The Lord told me that boy's going to be a preacher some day!"

Preaching must have been the Lord's will for my life, because He certainly knew that it wasn't mine. I didn't want to preach. My secret fear was that I would enter the ministry only to backslide again later and bring reproach upon the Lord. I was afraid that if I fell as a preacher, I would pull others down with me. I was afraid of the tremendous responsibility associated with the ministry.

But I had a very real burden for my generation. If I was indeed called to preach, then God would have to prove it to me. . . .

SIGNS FROM GOD

I had to be sure of the call to preach; I needed confirmation. So I asked God for a sign. One night after service, about a dozen of us stayed at church, talking and praying together until nearly midnight. It had been raining, and I went to the door to see if the rain had stopped. I had just prayed, "Lord, what do You want me to do with my life? If You are really calling me, I want to know. . . . "

And there it was! A burning bush!

Well, maybe not a bush—but a tree!

Just like Moses' burning bush, a tree in the yard outside the church appeared to be on fire but was not really burning up! I was amazed! After all, hadn't I just been reading about Moses and the burning bush in Exodus? The Scripture I had read came to mind immediately: "Go . . . set My people free!"

I rubbed my eyes. Could it be that I was witnessing such a miracle?

Wow, I thought. *This must be my sign from God!*

But then I went outside to investigate and discovered a trash can burning about a hundred yards away, barely visible behind the tree. *Someone has decided to burn their trash at midnight. What a coincidence.*

Oh, well, so much for my miracle sign from God. . . .

SIGNS AND WONDERS FOLLOWING

Maybe that was no burning bush I saw, and perhaps not even a burning tree. The zeal that burned within me was nevertheless real, but I still needed a sign. I went to see George. If George got saved, that would be sign enough for me.

Even after narrowly escaping with his life in the horrible accident we had both survived, George was still heavily involved in drugs and generally angry about everything. His parents had divorced over issues stemming from an extreme form of Pentecostalism.

George's father didn't believe in doctors. Once his mother took his brother to a doctor to have a knee injury diagnosed. George's dad went ballistic and tried to rip the stitches out of his son's knee "so God could heal it." To keep him from ripping the stitches out of his brother's knee, George's other brother got involved and engaged his father in a fistfight. Because of experiences like these, George had grown to hate Christianity.

You can easily see why George was not too thrilled when I "got religion." Now that I was out of the hospital, I went to see him every day, hoping he would one day come to the Lord.

One night on the way to see George I ran into the biggest drug dealer in the county and told him about Jesus. "Mike, I've found something that's better than those drugs you have!" Whether it was the fact that *I* said it, or whether he just couldn't believe that I had survived the car wreck, Mike listened as I told him what had happened to me since the accident. He listened as I told him about my miraculous healing and hastened recovery. Before we parted, I invited him to the revival at our church. In a few days he showed up at church, carrying a stash of sixteen tabs of LSD that he later confided he had planned to use to OD (overdose) and commit suicide. Instead, he gave his life to Christ.

When Mike got saved, I was so excited that I just knew I could finally use that fact to convince George to follow suit. One night around ten o'clock I again sought the Lord for George's salvation. "Whatever it takes to get George saved, Lord. . . . " I continued to pray for him, and then I asked God for a favor: "Will You save

George so I can use that as a sign that I am called to preach?"

George totaled his car the next day. He wasn't hurt, but a passenger, his girlfriend, had broken her collarbone. He went to pieces and began to cry. She tried to comfort him by saying, "Don't cry, George! God's with us!"

That night at church, in walked George. He had ridden to church with Mike. When the invitation was given following the sermon, George ran to the altar weeping and was gloriously saved.

But even George getting saved was not enough of a sign to make my confirmation into the ministry certain. It may have been a coincidence; after all, he had had two narrow escapes from death. I decided to ask God for another sign. A few days later our thirty-three-year-old music director had a stroke, which left him with some general weakness and limitations on the left side of his body, along with some swelling and pain in his hands.

I prayed, "Lord, if I'm called to preach, would You let him play the piano tomorrow night without any pain?" The next day I went over to see the music minister to check his progress; he was still unable to move his left hand without difficulty. So I figured I was safe.

But that night was something else. Before a packed auditorium with standing room only, our music director went to the piano and began to play in his own unique style as if nothing out of the ordinary had happened to him. I remember sitting there and thinking, *Hey, that sounds like Fred!* It *was* Fred.

Sure enough, there was Fred, playing the piano—with both hands—beautifully as ever. When he was finished playing, Fred found his way over to the pew right in front of mine and sat down. I tapped him on the shoulder and said, "Fred, I want to ask you a question: Did you have any pain while you were playing?"

"No," he answered. "I felt that I heard the Holy Spirit say to me, 'If you go to the piano and play, I'll heal you.' And as soon as my hands hit the keyboard, all the movement came back, all the swelling went out of my hands, and all the pain left."

I was absolutely in awe. Right there, right then, I was certain God had called me into the ministry. I quickly stood to my feet.

The pastor saw me and recognized me to speak. I told everyone present that night, "I want to acknowledge that God has called me to preach!"

At that, one of the trustees of the church—a big, burly railroad worker—rose to his feet and said, "Brother Randy, we've known that for a couple of weeks! We've just been waiting for you to announce it!"

TWO

PREACHING

I will lead the blind by ways they have not known, along un-familiar paths I will guide them; I will turn the darkness into light before them and make the rough places smooth. These are the things I will do; I will not forsake them.

—ISAIAH 42:16

I STARTED TO WORK for God practically the minute I answered the call to preach. I remember being absolutely on fire with this zeal to reach the lost—especially those of my age group, the Baby Boomers as we were called. I was involved in youth ministry at our church and even began to preach weekend revivals as the doors to do so were opened. I had already seen the power of God on enough occasions to know He could heal. And if He could heal, what about all those many other miracles mentioned in the Bible?

I believed in the whole Bible—miracles and all. But I knew I still had a lot to learn before God would release me into the ministry He had called me to. How was I to know that there would be many storms ahead—many trials, tests, heartbreaks, disappointments, and persecutions before I would be given the green light to preach—finally!

But all I could see in the midst of my passion to serve the God I loved was a bright future that would no doubt be spent pastoring one of the largest churches in the General Baptist denomination. As I prayed for guidance, I began to feel a very strong leading to enroll in Oakland City College and major in religious studies. *Now that would require a miracle—maybe more than just one!*

My mom and dad had taken a bath in a bad business deal that resulted in near bankruptcy the year before. I had saved some money, but only enough to attend one quarter of college. Instead of enrolling in the state school that was quite inexpensive, I wanted to go to a denominational school and study for the ministry. Dad was still struggling financially, and I knew my parents would not be able to help me. I did the only thing I knew to do; I prayed, "Lord, if You want me to go to ministry school, You'll make a way."

And so He did. The Lord worked miraculously, giving me scholarships and grants to enable me to go all the way through four years of college and three years of seminary, owing virtually nothing for that education. He paid for all of it!

I entered Oakland City College in January 1971 and majored in religion. My first year there, I preached approximately twenty weekend revivals in Kentucky, Indiana, Illinois, and Michigan. My pastor, who was still Brother Bill Duncan, introduced me to a man named Leo Walton. Leo, an evangelist, had been Brother Duncan's pastor. He and his wife, Rose, taught me much about prayer and ministry.

A MIGHTY MAN OF GOD

Before coming to know the Lord, Leo Walton had been a businessman, a drunkard, a gambler, and a fighter. He came to church on crutches the night he was saved. At first he had trouble believing that a sinner such as he was would ever be completely forgiven, until a friend of his asked, "Leo, would you be willing to preach?"

He responded, "I'd do anything—even preach—if God would just save me!" Instantly the guilt departed as the power of God hit him. The Holy Spirit came upon him. He jumped up, threw his crutches down, picked Rose up in his arms, and danced around the room with her. Formerly a Catholic, Leo had found Christ at a Baptist revival.

Leo had had an egg business. When his suppliers, mostly Catholics, discovered that he had gotten saved at a Baptist meeting, they refused to sell him their eggs. He lost his business but gained Christ.

Supernatural manifestations of the power of God occurred almost immediately in Leo's life. For instance, while driving, Leo would glance at road signs along the way; instead of flashy advertisements for cigarettes, motels, or beer, he would see Scripture verses written across the poles. Even stranger, he would miraculously see signs on poles that had no billboards attached to them at all—just bare poles, the kind that carry raw power or phone lines from town to town. Leo had yet another problem; he couldn't read. But when those Scripture signs appeared, he could both read and comprehend them. He learned to read by those Bible signs along the roadside that were visible only to him. When he returned home, he opened the Bible to the passage he had seen on the pole, and his wife read the words to him. Leo Walton was used mightily by God all across southern Illinois and southern Indiana in the years to come.

When I met Leo he was elderly and homebound. Because he had been a drunkard in his younger days, he suffered from cirrhosis of the liver and an enlarged heart. But he and Rose were still people of prayer. I would sit for hours, just listening to them teach me about prayer and preaching. Then Leo would ask, "Where are you preaching next?" I'd tell him about my next meeting, and he would respond, "I'll pray for you, brother!"

At one of the early revivals, someone even said to me after I was finished preaching, "You remind me of Leo Walton! The same anointing is on you that is on him." That was a tremendous compliment, then as now.

My ongoing interest in faith and healing was further

stimulated when Leo told me of the miraculous healing of his daughter, who had become gravely ill during the early years of his ministry. She was comatose and suffering from a high fever. The doctor had come to the house and told Leo that she needed to be moved to a hospital, but he had neither money nor insurance. After the doctor left, Leo knelt down by his daughter's bedside and began to intercede for her. He lost track of time, but after awhile he felt someone's hand touch his head. It was the hand of his daughter; the fever had broken, and she had awakened from the coma. As he looked up at her, she asked, "Daddy, what is wrong? Why are you crying?"

The Waltons had a great influence upon my life, for which I am especially grateful. We can learn from those who have gone before us. We can greatly benefit from their spiritual wisdom and experience. Even though God may be doing a new thing in our lives and ministries, there is still much benefit in listening to—and learning from—the Leo Waltons of this world. . . .

HAPPILY EVER AFTER . . . ?

In July 1971 I got married—on the rebound after hearing about Doris's engagement to another guy. I was just nineteen, but I thought marriage was the right thing to do at the time—that it was exactly what I needed. Little did I know that one person, much less two, could barely live off the minuscule offerings I received preaching at weekend revival meetings. A good week's income was a mere fifty dollars.

I still wanted to reach my generation, and I remember telling my dad, "When I start preaching, I'm not going to wear a suit. I'm going to preach in bell-bottom blue jeans and tie-dyed shirts." But soon after my marriage, I discovered that not many people of my generation even attended church or were in positions of power and influence. The older generation didn't seem to understand my blue jeans and tie-dyed shirts. If I wanted to preach, I would have to wear a suit. So I did what I had to do in order to preach and tried to relate the best way I could to my generation while working within the confines of those set boundaries.

My monthly income the first year was somewhere around two hundred dollars. This sum had to pay for the books and part of my college tuition not covered by grants and scholarships, as well as cover living expenses for two. That put all kinds of pressure on me, as you can well imagine. But pressure is the method God uses to forge His plans and shape us into that which He always intended us to be from that which falls pitifully short in most respects. As I look back today over this early period of my adult life, I can see the Master Potter's hands at work, forming me. I can see His purpose, so that I can now say, "You are our Father; we are the clay, and You our potter; and all we are the work of Your hand" (Isa. 64:8, NKJV).

While those of us from small towns in southern Illinois were not the best educated, we possessed a deep faith that no amount of intellectual knowledge could replace. That foundation of faith held fast and remained firm in me, even after I added education to it and was exposed to liberal theological views during seminary. I have since discovered that God uses everything—all our joys, all our sorrows, all our strengths and weaknesses, all our successes, and even our failures.

And all the time, when the storms came and the pressures hit, God was molding His values and His truth into my life by His very hands. He taught me the value of commitment, unity, and the supernatural dimension of the Christian faith. All these truths were made real to me during this shaping process. I know I was merely the clay in His hands—clay He used to shape and transform me into someone He could eventually use. . . .

But before He could use me, this clay vessel known as Randy Clark would have to go through the fire.

REFINING FIRE

My marriage was falling apart. It seemed that no matter how hard I tried, no matter how hard I prayed, I couldn't prevent the inevitable—divorce. To this day, I consider my first marriage and eventual divorce to be the biggest failure of my life.

We were having serious arguments by the third day of our

honeymoon. If I had not been a pastor, I would have ended the marriage by having it annulled the first month. By then, I knew we were in trouble. Because we were in the ministry, we tried to make it work. But it was difficult for both of us. It was a time of great emotional trauma.

I prayed constantly for God to help me love my wife even when she was saying and doing some very unlovely things to me. Even though now I realize that she struck out at me as a result of the hurts and wounds she had experienced even before our marriage, at the time I had much trouble dealing with her temperament. Her father owned a gun and I was told that he had once fired it in the home in anger. It became obvious to me that my wife had married me in order to escape the hell that had been her life. On the other hand, I married her because I was young . . . and because I did not heed the advice of many people who loved me, including that of my parents and best friends.

During our three-year marriage, we went through two years of counseling with two of my professors at school. Our home life was very dysfunctional. I had come from a peaceful home where I had never seen my parents argue. Now I found myself immersed in a tumultuous lifestyle much like the one my wife had been trying to escape. Our home was filled with continual bickering punctuated by bitter arguments.

Another thing was happening to me: My theological views were changing. Radically.

No Longer a "Fighting, Feuding, Fundamentalist"

That's what they called us back in southern Illinois—"fighting, feuding, fundamentalists." But while my marriage was falling down around my ears, I began to be influenced by a very loving—and very liberal—professor whose theological views were very different from those that I had been raised to believe were absolutely true and unwavering. I entered a period of "non-religious influence" that made me more and more open to the views my professor expressed to me. I became very liberal theologically for a period of time—even to the point of disbelieving in the devil or his demons. And if I had not experienced God's power to heal at age eighteen, I would have let go of that belief, too.

I have had to overcome much skepticism imparted to me by the years I spent undergoing theological training at college and seminary. Now I can admit that I wish I had had a very conservative theological training, as it would have made the faith walk easier for me to understand and develop. Instead, all that liberal theology changed me into a revisionist, for at least a period of time. I may not have even been aware of what was happening to me, but those around me could see how much my theology had changed.

At one point when my marriage was especially stormy, Dr. Smith, one of my favorite professors, asked me, "Randy, do you know your views are changing? If you go back to southern Illinois now, you're going to be hurt by the church. Do you love the church enough to serve it . . . even when it hurts?"

At the time, I paid little attention to his remarks. I had been very popular as a young preacher, and I was well-liked. In fact, my pastor had been preparing me to take his place. I sincerely believed that I was being groomed to pastor the largest church in our Baptist association. I had received nothing but praise and accolades. Yet I did take my professor's gentle warning somewhat to heart, because he had been the first Baptist pastor in the state of Mississippi to be kicked out of the pulpit in his church after his deacons had asked him, "Dr. Smith, what would you do if a black man wanted to join this church?"

"I should have been content to let sleeping dogs lie," he related to me many years afterward. "But I couldn't dodge the question. So I answered: 'If you close the doors of this church to any man because of the color of his skin, it's the same as closing the doors to Jesus Christ.'"

The deacon board responded almost immediately with this edict: "You've got thirty days to get yourself and your family out of the parsonage. You're fired." Here was a man who had nurtured the church, who had brought it from a scant few members to a weekly attendance of more than seven hundred, who had worked so hard to make it grow that he had suffered a near-fatal heart attack. Now he was out of a job—just like that.

27

That one thing made me seriously consider his remarks before I responded: "Sure, I love the church of Jesus Christ enough to serve it, even when it hurts." It wasn't long before I would find out exactly what that comment would cost me.

A MARKED MAN

After three years of marriage, my wife and I were separated. During our separation, I was told by a credible source that my wife was having an affair. This revelation ended my hope for the marriage. I asked her for a divorce, citing unfaithfulness. She filed for divorce on the grounds of irreconcilable differences.

The divorce proceedings rolled ahead, full speed. The consequences began almost immediately, making me a marked man within my own denomination—where divorced men were given no opportunity to minister.

When I registered at the Southern Baptist Theological Seminary in Louisville, Kentucky, I mentioned on the entrance questionnaire that I was "going through a divorce." Nobody said anything to me. Somehow, somebody missed picking up on this one important detail, and I was allowed to enter.

During my first year there, all the students were given the Minnesota Multiphasic Personality Inventory, which consisted of about five hundred questions. When my results came in, the dean of students invited me to his office to discuss them: "We have some problems here, Clark," he said, with a serious look on his face. "Some of these answers you gave just don't seem to fit together. For example, this test shows that you should be on the verge of a nervous breakdown, but you're not. How do you explain this?"

If that were true—and I believed it was—I certainly showed no visible outward signs of such a nervous disorder. The dean asked me to explain why it was that outwardly I appeared to be so cool when, in fact, I was being tossed about by inner storms.

"Well, sir, I am nearing the end of my divorce proceedings," I began. "In a few weeks, the divorce will be final."

"Divorce? *What divorce?*" the dean inquired, by now visibly disturbed at what he was hearing.

I explained to him some of the highlights of the turmoil my marriage had produced—including a horrible argument that had so upset me my muscles began to twitch and spasm uncontrollably. Every muscle in my body was out of control, and I thought I was losing it emotionally. I feared that I would break into a million pieces, but somehow I was able to dial the phone and call for help. Some friends came right over to pray for me, and the muscle spasms stopped as the peace of God floated down over me.

"Even if my divorce means that I'll be disqualified from ministry, I have no choice," I told the dean of students. "My marriage cannot be saved. If I'm close to a nervous breakdown, the only reason I haven't had it is that I have decided not to have one. I have gone through the grieving process of ending my marriage for the past year, and I have just decided that I'm going to deal with it, not break down."

My ministry had been the sole reason we had stayed together as long as we had; it had become all too apparent that even ministry would not provide enough glue to keep the marriage together. I still remember how it felt to be told for the first time, "Someone who's divorced is through with ministry." It hit me like a cold shower or a slap in the face.

Now the dean was asking, "What do you think we ought to do with you?"

I related to him that I had been told that a divorced person could go to seminary at Southern Baptist Theological Seminary. He said, "You have been given some wrong information. It's true that one can enter the school if he has been through a divorce and has remarried; however, if one is divorced while still in school, he must leave."

I left seminary at the end of the semester. Some of the dean's last few words of advice to me were, "You're a bright student; enter law school. Don't come back."

And his last word—period—was even more ominous: "You'll never have a ministry."

As far as pastoring that big Baptist church was concerned, it was painfully apparent to me that it was never going to happen. I was divorced. As far as the Baptists were concerned, that made me a marked man—a man marked with the word *failure*.

"YOU'LL NEVER HAVE A MINISTRY!"

Over and over the dean's words rang through my head. Like bells, they clanged against my tattered nerves, chiding, *"You'll never have a ministry! You'll never have a ministry!* All of this has been for nothing! You've blown it! You'll never amount to anything in God's kingdom—or on earth!"

What could I do? I had burned all my bridges. In college I had studied nothing but religion because I sincerely believed that the rest of my life would be spent pastoring churches. I had purposely stacked my credits in the direction of theology and religion because I didn't want to be tempted later to go the bivocational route and become itinerant, floating in and out of ministry. I really wanted to work in full-time ministry. In fact, I didn't want to do anything but preach. And now that wasn't possible.

I was badly burned and soon became bitter—so bitter that for several weeks I experienced another bout of backsliding. I began to drink, despite the fact that I didn't even like the taste of alcohol and had only had one drink in my life prior to this period of time. I also fell into a brief period of sexual immorality, due in part to the influence of liberal theology that I had come under while in seminary. I couldn't stand the guilt, however, and cried out to God to get me back on track spiritually. There I was, twenty-two, divorced, and riddled by guilt over my backslidden condition because of all the pain the divorce had caused.

After a night of drinking, I returned to the apartment I shared with another couple, depressed, angry, and disillusioned. Dr. Smith's question flooded back into my mind as if right on cue: "Randy, do you love the church of Jesus Christ enough to serve it even when it hurts?" In spite of my alcohol haze, deep conviction dropped down over me, and I fell to my knees and said, "Yes, Lord! Forgive me for blaming You! I'll serve You even when it hurts!"

I suddenly realized that I had become angry at God both

because of all the hurt I had been experiencing from my divorce and because of being rejected and kicked out of seminary. Suddenly I came to my senses as it became obvious to me that God didn't feel that way about me. He was not the one who had hurt me. In the past few months I had told people again and again, "I'll never pastor! I'll never have a church! I'll never have a ministry!" I repented of making those statements too and then asked God to heal my many hurts.

Finally I told the Lord, "If You want me to go back to seminary, I will go. But if I never go back to seminary and never pastor a big Baptist church, I will still follow You! If I have to pump gas and pastor at a tiny church somewhere out in the sticks, I'll still follow You! *I will serve You no matter what!* I surrender all to You!"

As I did, the grace of God fell from heaven, and I was covered with an unmistakable, almost indescribable peace. I began to discover the reality of Isaiah 40:29–31: "He gives strength to the weary and increases the power of the weak. Even youths grow tired and weary, and young men stumble and fall; but those who hope in the LORD will renew their strength. They will soar on wings like eagles; they will run and not grow weary, they will walk and not be faint."

That night I put my faith in the belief that, divorce and all, God still loved me and had not lifted the call on my life. I committed to pursue my ministry full speed ahead and not to listen to those who told me that it was no use even to think about the ministry.

That night God got hold of my heart—all of it—and He has never let go, not once.

PUTTING IT BACK TOGETHER

I had scattered little pieces of myself all over the highway of life during that period of depression and despair. The night I surrendered everything to God was a turning point in my life. Now the Lord was ministering to me on a very deep level to put me back together again. It took nearly two years to work through all the hurts and pain, and for the next ten years I cried out almost daily, asking God to forgive me for that brief period of back-sliding that had produced such overwhelming guilt within me. I kept telling Him how sorry I was for my sins. I knew I was for-given, but it still felt good to tell God how sorry I was that I had slipped and fallen. Even to this day, I remind God how thankful I am that He reached down during this dark period of my life and pulled me out of the trenches of despair.

Again and again I found myself on my knees, calling out for more of God's grace just to make it through the day. And He seemed to be answering: "My grace is sufficient for you, for my power is made perfect in weakness" (2 Cor. 12:9).

It seemed that my life was on a course of its own as I wound up back in McLeansboro, Illinois, where I had gone to work for my grandpa Clark. Now there I was, driving a semitruck to help him out after he had a heart attack—and to help myself out, because my wife had run up all my credit cards, which I was still responsible for paying off.

I spent a lot of time on the road, and I used that time to think about my life and its direction.

McLeansboro, the county seat, is a small town, population twenty-six hundred. Almost no one I had gone to school with still lived around there—no one except for a girl named DeAnne Davenport whom I had known in high school. DeAnne lived in Eldorado, Illinois, about twenty miles away. As teenagers we had double-dated a couple of times when she was going steady with my best friend, Joe Barker. But then Joe was killed, and I lost all track of DeAnne.

On a whim one evening, I phoned her to talk over old times and to see what God was doing in her life, if anything at all. As a result of that phone call, we got together and started dating. DeAnne was just as beautiful as ever, and I wanted to be with her every chance I had. So we dated every night for the next six months, except for the three nights I was snowed in at a truck stop in Chicago.

DeAnne had been converted to Christ during the revival in which I was called to preach. She had not been raised in a Christian home but had experienced one year of being on fire for God following the revival, only to grow cool once more as she fell out of fellowship with Christians after moving to the St. Louis area. When we discussed her spiritual condition, she admitted to me that she knew that she was not where she ought to be with the Lord.

I really wanted to marry DeAnne, but I told her that our getting married was useless unless her relationship with God was restored. To her credit, DeAnne was very honest with me—honest enough to tell me that she was open to rededicating her life to Christ, but that it would have to be by the leading of the Holy Spirit, not by her own efforts.

"I can't make the changes on my own," she said quite frankly. Openness and honesty are just a few of the traits I love most about DeAnne. She was a breath of fresh air to me. . . . still is. I admired the fact that whatever happened, DeAnne wanted to hear directly from God for herself. So I prayed for her that the Lord would convict her of her sins and that the Holy Spirit would draw her into a genuine work of rededication.

Within one month, while I preached a weekend revival at a small church in Blairsville, Illinois, she rededicated her life to Christ. The powerful work of the Holy Spirit had begun in DeAnne's life. We became engaged.

MORE SETBACKS

The summer before I married DeAnne, I spoke at the Mount Olivet Association of General Baptists' Sunday School Convention, as well as at the presbytery meeting. In addition, I held revival meetings at two of the largest churches in the association. In the first presbytery meeting, which I did not attend, a motion was brought to have my ordination revoked.

The presbytery was basing its recommendation on a ruling that stated that a man could not be ordained if he had two living wives. This rule interpreted the act of divorce as not being valid to dissolve a marriage in the eyes of God and the church. It also interpreted the passage in 1 Timothy 3:1–7— that a man in pastoral positions must be "blameless, the husband of one wife" (NKJV)—to connote divorce rather than polygamy, which was known to have been practiced in biblical times.

I felt as if I had once again been stabbed in the back. Why had no one prepared me for this procedure by telling me about it face-to-face before the meeting had taken place? Why had this even happened, since I had been assured by the person in charge of the credentials committee that the dissolution of my first marriage would not be a problem to my remaining ordained by the committee?

Apparently he had been wrong in his appraisal. My hopes for pastoring took another nosedive.

DeAnne and I arranged to meet with a committee from the presbytery, and I was advised to state the circumstances that led to my divorce. I refused to do this because I believed that nothing would be accomplished by it.

Since my first wife's parents, and mine, were members of the same church, I chose not to go that route. My former wife and I had been through enough. I told the committee that if they would leave me alone for six months, I would voluntarily leave the denomination. This move, I believed, would prevent the potential of a major controversy arising regarding my divorce and recent remarriage. Besides, the presbytery meeting to rule on this was to be held in my home church where my parents and former in-laws attended.

Nevertheless, the position these men took still made no sense to me. For me, it was no longer a question of whether or not I could be in ministry; it was a question of whether or not I could be a church member or, for that matter, a Christian.

The logical conclusion that everyone seemed to draw was that, although I had biblical reasons for my divorce, I would be committing adultery once I remarried. I was left to choose between the American Baptists and the United Methodists for my credentials to preach.

After much prayer and soul-searching, I left the General Baptists and turned to the American Baptists for a place to minister, primarily because I did not favor the Episcopal form of government practiced by the United Methodists.

A Second Chance at Love

Falling in love with DeAnne is the second-best thing that ever happened to me, right after falling in love with Jesus. She was—and is—my second chance at love. She is my best friend and helpmate. DeAnne Davenport and I were married July 12, 1975, and it still seems like yesterday.

During the first two and one-half years of our marriage I returned to the Southern Baptist Theological Seminary—and life was great. I received a student pastorate at an American Baptist church in Greensburg, Indiana. DeAnne and I were so in love that once a youth at the church was overheard saying, "Man, when I get married I want a marriage like Randy and DeAnne Clark's! I've never seen a happier couple!"

Our financial picture was just as tight as it had been during my first marriage, but DeAnne and I were happy. Our life together was wonderful. I cleared just over two thousand dollars for the year 1976 after car expenses. DeAnne's parents helped us out with food. Sometimes we'd have just enough cash to buy gas to drive to church in order to get paid again, so we could drive back home. In spite of all the difficulties, we were happy and blessed.

After graduation I took a pastorate at an American Baptist church in Spillertown, in southern Illinois. The interim pastor had introduced me to the congregation, and I was excited to be given the opportunity to serve from the pulpit. I expected a smooth transition; boy, was I wrong!

The interim pastor, one of the two counselors I had met with for two years during my first marriage, immediately disclosed that I had been divorced. Upon meeting with the board of deacons, I asked the six men present, "If I am called to preach here, will you be able to serve with me, knowing that I have been divorced?" Each one answered to the affirmative, and I came highly recommended by the interim pastor, Jim McDannel.

But it soon became apparent that not all of the deacons were equally enthusiastic about having me as their pastor. Two of the men openly resisted me to the point that one day I asked them, "Why did you tell me you could serve with me? If you had answered *no,* I would not have even considered accepting this pastorate!"

The two men replied in unison, "We didn't want to hurt your feelings."

Well, my feelings were certainly hurt now—as were DeAnne's. One of the men continued, "We didn't think you'd get the call, and so we didn't say anything. We didn't think you had a chance anyway."

Three of the deacons resigned. One reconsidered, returned, and fought me for the next year. The Sunday school superintendent resigned in an uproar; the youth fellowship director resigned, and so did the choir director. DeAnne and I had stepped into quite a mess, and it was much harder on her than it was on me. She had not been raised in a church environment and had never witnessed some of the behavior that we now had to contend with almost daily from brothers and sisters in Christ.

A great deal of bitterness was directed at me by members of the congregation because I had been divorced and remarried. Those were three years of hell for us. It was not unusual for DeAnne to be sitting in the sanctuary and be able to hear people arguing from behind the closed doors of the pastoral offices. The arguments often involved me and an upset member of the congregation. Once a man came to our home to give me a piece of his mind. As he addressed me from outside the doorway where we stood, there was so much anger loaded into his voice that DeAnne could hear him shouting from inside the house—even with all the doors and windows shut tight.

My otherwise idyllic second marriage was feeling the stress and strain of all the church turmoil. DeAnne became severely wounded. She had actually thought that all Christians were supposed to love each other! What a rude awakening all this bitter business was to her. She said, "If this is what church life is all about, I want nothing to do with it!" And she meant it. She began to distance herself from church. She got a job and even agreed to work Sundays so she would not have to endure the things she saw and heard at church during that period of so much infighting.

Once after I returned home from a meeting I had attended in Wisconsin, DeAnne met me at the door and said, "Randy, we have to talk. I can't take any more of this! I want a divorce. I can't stay married to you because I can't handle the ministry."

But the idea of another divorce was devastating to me. I told her, "No! We'll do whatever it takes to work this out. If I have to resign this church and take a secular job for awhile, I'll do it. Just don't leave. I know God has put us together!"

"I love you, Randy," she told me with tears streaming down her face. "I'm afraid that I can't be a good pastor's wife. You need somebody who's better at it than me."

But I knew all I needed was DeAnne. She stayed.

ONE MORE TRY . . .

I had been given an opportunity to take a pastorate in Wisconsin. On the surface, it looked like the right thing to do—more money, no strife; why not? But as I prayed, I knew in my heart that the Lord was not ready to release me from Spillertown Baptist Church.

I told the deacons who had fought me so fervently for the past three years, "I believe the Lord wants me to stay in Spillertown; but if I stay, you'll have to make the decision for me. You'll have to vote for me to stay. And if I stay, I want no more power struggles. I want the power to lead. I have earned the right to fail . . . or succeed. And if you men can't work with me, then resign and let me appoint some men who can."

To my surprise, that is exactly what happened. I stayed for the next four years and enjoyed the new freedom of leadership that resulted from that truth session with the deacons. But for DeAnne, the damage had already been done. She was still too wounded to enjoy this new period of freedom in our lives.

Even though DeAnne remained distanced from church, the Lord brought us through. All the while I was praying, "Lord, deal with DeAnne. Touch her. Bring her back into fellowship with Christians. Restore her! Here I am, trying to get closer to You, and she's slipping farther away. I'm afraid that if this continues much longer, it will destroy our marriage!"

ALL THINGS MADE NEW

God heard my desperate prayers, and within three months DeAnne was restored by His gracious hand. He had not only answered my prayers; He had done exceedingly abundantly above all I could ask or think! We were happier than ever, as if all those bitter exchanges that had driven DeAnne away from Spillertown Baptist Church had never even taken place.

And I began to realize that through all the turmoil God had been teaching me some very specific lessons. First, I learned that serving God could be very painful at times. I also learned about the wicked contents of my own heart and about my propensity to fall into sin. I learned some things about the vulnerability of those who have been divorced and the often unfair treatment they receive at the hands of Christians who do not understand the reasons their marriages failed or the depths of their subsequent pain. I learned not to react negatively toward God because of the unfair ways others treated me. I learned that if a pastor who is a husband is not careful, the ministry can destroy his wife. I learned to be willing to suffer for Christ's sake.

I also learned that the church can be very hateful, as well as very loving. And I learned to love the church . . . even when it hurt.

THREE

PRESSING IN

But when he, the Spirit of truth, comes, he will guide you into all truth. He will not speak on his own; he will speak only what he hears, and he will tell you what is yet to come.
—JOHN 16:13

N O QUESTION ABOUT IT: I knew there was more to walking with God than I had been experiencing. I found that out by accident one afternoon in the summer of 1983. I was sitting at my desk in the new educational building we had just built and I was praying: "Lord, thank You that I'm no longer liberal in my thinking or someone who doesn't believe You did all those miraculous things in the Bible! Lord, I believe You did everything the Bible says You did! All those wonderful things like turning water to wine and making blind people see—those are not myths or legends. You did those things. Lord, I'm glad I'm not a cessationist—someone who believes You did miraculous things in the past but that You no longer do them. I thank You for that!"

Does that prayer sound as Pharisaical to you as it now does to me? But that was the best I could do in the summer of 1983, when in response to that somewhat pompous prayer I heard an inward voice reply, *"So what?"*

Very clearly, very unmistakably, I had heard it: *"So what?"* It shocked me so much to hear that question that I began to listen for more. . . .

In a few moments another statement came on the heels of the first: "You might as well be a liberal or a cessationist. You say that you believe I do all these things and that you even believe in the gifts; yet you don't know how to move in them."

At that point, I was so shaken that I responded, "Lord, I'm willing to learn!"

So I began pressing in, in prayer. I also did a lot of reading. I went out and bought seven hundred dollars' worth of books on everything I could find that had to do with the Holy Spirit and the manifestation of spiritual gifts. I read about the baptism of the Holy Spirit. I read the views on the Holy Spirit expressed by the Pentecostals, the Faith camp, the charismatic Roman Catholics, the Episcopalians—and everything in between. I virtually read any book about the Holy Spirit that I could get my hands on.

About a week after I had bought all those books and begun to read them, a young man came to my church to preach. A graduate of the same Baptist college I had attended, he spoke to us about the woman with the issue of blood. I had heard sermons before on this topic. In fact, I had even preached on this passage from the Bible. But I always spiritualized it and never dealt with the actual issue of healing. I dealt with the woman's faith and how God had faithfully met her need. But I had never taken the literal approach—that Jesus had, in fact, healed this woman who had persevered and pressed through the crowd to receive her miracle. I had never focused on her faith for healing—and neither was this young preacher. He too was spiritualizing the text.

Yet, as I listened to this man preach, I began to cry. Hot tears gushed out of my eyes, and I became concerned about what was happening to me as I sat there, an emotional mess, thinking, *What's going on here? What's happening to me? This is not that emotional of a sermon. Lord, what are You doing?* The answer came in a series of three strong impressions that hit me—Bam! Bam! Bam!

"I want you to teach this church that I still heal today.

"I want you to have a conference on healing at this church.

"I want you to preach differently."

A Divine Appointment

To have a conference on healing at my church meant that God would have to send someone to lead it, since I had not yet been instructed in the operation of the gifts of the Holy Spirit. Who could I invite to come to conduct such a conference? Then I thought of calling a friend of mine, Larry Hart, an associate professor and chaplain at Oral Roberts University in Tulsa, Oklahoma.

"Larry," I asked, "would you come and teach us about healing? And can you bring Francis MacNutt or Morton Kelsey?"

Larry said he would be delighted to come and suggested bringing someone he knew quite well—John Wimber.

"I've never heard of John Wimber," I responded. "Let me pray about it."

"Fine, you pray about it and let me know," said Larry.

Perhaps he could tell by my tone of voice that deep down I wasn't very open to the idea of his bringing John Wimber. But my attitude was about to change.

The next morning, I was walking past a television in our home. It was tuned to a local Christian station that carried TBN's *Praise the Lord* program. I happened to overhear Paul Crouch in the midst of introducing a big, teddy bear of a man who looked a little like Kenny Rogers. What he was saying about this man so intrigued me that I had to stop and listen. As he was expressing some of this man's views on the subject of healing, I was really hooked. *Who is this guy?* I wondered, as Paul Crouch took his time delivering a lengthy discourse before announcing the visitor's name.

Then he said, "It's our privilege to have John Wimber with us. Please join me in giving him a warm *Praise the Lord* welcome!"

I was stunned! *That's who Larry wants to bring to our conference!*

I taped the program to play back later when I met with the board of deacons who were assisting in planning the conference. Immediately after we viewed the tape, I called John Wimber and invited him to speak at our healing conference. He said he couldn't come then, but he could send a team in March 1984.

Before that time there was much to do. I had to prepare our deacons and the congregation for the conference by teaching them the foundations of biblical healing and the gifts of the Holy Spirit. But first I had to learn them for myself. . . .

GOD'S SCHOOL

Did you know that the Holy Spirit has His own school? When we get serious about Him, He becomes serious about assuming His role as our Teacher, the Third Person of the Trinity, who guides us "into all truth" (John 16:13). As I kept pressing in to know more about the Holy Spirit and His gifts, I began to learn about them in strange and unusual ways. It was during an ordinary awards ceremony given by the Great Rivers Region of the American Baptist Churches U.S.A. in 1983 that I had my first instruction about the gift the Bible calls the "word of knowledge." I had been invited to attend because our church won the region's Evangelism Award that year. I was there to accept it. During the event I met a woman pastor who had graduated from a seminary in St. Louis and earned a doctor of ministry degree. In the course of our conversation, she mentioned that she flowed in the gift of the word of knowledge. So I asked her, "How do you know when that gift is in operation?"

I'll never forget what she said: "Honey, I just check my body out before I go into the service." By that, she explained, she checked to see if she was experiencing any pain—sympathetic pain. I didn't understand what she was talking about . . . until weeks later.

About a month later I was praying about a woman in my congregation who had recently discovered that she had cancer. I was very disturbed to find this out, because this woman was very respected and had been a member of our church for many years. The deacons and I had prayed for her again and again, but we didn't seem to be making any headway. Although the team from John Wimber's church was scheduled to hold their healing conference in a few months, I felt that this situation should not wait. So I phoned his church, the Vineyard in Yorba Linda, California, and requested that someone instruct me about how to pray effectively for this woman's healing. I was finally able to reach Lance Pittluck, then an intern at the Vineyard in Yorba Linda and now overseer for the Vineyard's New York region. Lance had been trained as a Presbyterian.

"Do you have words of knowledge?" he asked me.

"I believe in them," I answered, a bit hesitantly. "But personally I don't know anything about them."

Then Lance Pittluck proceeded to share with me the different church views concerning the gift of the word of knowledge, not all of them necessarily straight from the pages of the Bible. But, he added, the Vineyard had completed a lot of interviews with people who functioned in that gift with the evidence of fruit, and they said that they had found at least five primary ways for people to experience a word of knowledge:

1. By identifying sympathetic pain.
2. Through impressions.
3. By seeing words superimposed over the people for whom they were praying, as if the words had been written by an invisible hand.
4. By seeing visions or scenarios in their minds featuring the person they were praying for, in which they visualized the particular organ or limb that was affected with sickness or disease.
5. By speaking out some word about the condition the sick person was suffering from.

That fifth form, Pittluck said, was called "automatic speech." (I prefer to call it "inspired speech.")

In summary, he said, "A word of knowledge is as simple as this: You can feel it, know it, read it, see it, or say it." I wrote that information down on a file card and tucked it away.

The following Sunday night I had my first word of knowledge. It came while I was praying at the altar. As the leadership and I held hands and prayed for a young man who could not come to church because of severe back pain, my left eye started to hurt for a split second. The pain was so intense that I thought, *God? Are You trying to tell me something? Am I having a word of knowledge? If I am and I don't give it, then somebody could miss a healing. If I'm not and I'm missing You, then I could lose all the respect of this congregation—respect that I worked hard to get.*

What a dilemma!

As I struggled within me to know what to do with that pain in my left eye, this thought struck me: *Well, if I give this word and nobody responds I'll just look foolish. All I'll lose is my pride. But if I give it and it's right, God could heal somebody. I'm going to take the chance!*

Cautiously, I went over to the pulpit microphone and stammered out, "If . . . uh . . . someone of you . . . uh, possibly has something wrong with their left eye, well . . . uh . . . if you'll just come forward, we will pray for you." In a matter of minutes, a woman that I knew as Ruth was standing at the altar. An older, retired woman, Ruth was known among the congregation for being very strong-willed and unemotional. When her husband died of cancer she had hardly shed a tear. We gathered around Ruth and prayed for her, although none of us yet had had any training as to how to pray for the sick. We just recalled what Scripture said to do and anointed Ruth with oil, laid hands on her, and prayed. We prayed until everyone had run out of things to say, and then we stopped. Immediately when we stopped praying, Ruth commented, "Brother Randy, if you had not stopped praying when you did, I think I would have fallen on the floor. I was beginning to feel faint, and I thought I was going to fall down!"

Now I had also never seen anyone "slain in the Spirit," so the natural man in me leapt to the conclusion that poor posture and possibly having locked her knees had weakened her so she felt as if she would fall—just from standing in one place for too long. I had no comprehension that the Spirit of God had fallen on her. The good news is that she was healed of a condition—tunnel vision—that had affected the vision in her left eye. She had only a limited path of vision in her left eye—a small square of eyesight surrounded by darkness. That evening God gave her two good eyes. And He gave me the encouragement necessary to believe Him for the rest of what He had for me.

PRESSURE FROM ON HIGH

Discovering that you have just received a word of knowledge can really put the pressure on you—pressure from without, pressure from within, and pressure from on high. As the natural man fights for the right to look nice and dignified in front of a crowd of friends and total strangers, the enemy is pounding from without, "Don't do it! You're going to look stupid! Don't say anything!" But God keeps pouring on the pressure from on high, and pretty soon you're not just under the gun to give that word of knowledge; you're sweating bullets.

Is it God?

Is it not God?

Is it just coincidence?

These questions were rolling in my spirit as I decided that I would teach the whole church about what had happened to me during that Sunday night service when Ruth was healed of tunnel vision. At least that way, we would all be sweating bullets together!

The following Sunday I taught from 1 Corinthians, chapter 12, on words of knowledge:

> Now about spiritual gifts, brothers, I do not want you to be ignorant. You know that when you were pagans, somehow or other you were influenced and led astray to mute idols. Therefore I tell you that no one who is speaking by the Spirit of God says, "Jesus be cursed," and no one can say,

"Jesus is Lord," except by the Holy Spirit.

There are different kinds of gifts, but the same Spirit. There are different kinds of service, but the same Lord. There are different kinds of working, but the same God works all of them in all men.

Now to each man the manifestation of the Spirit is given for the common good. To one there is given through the Spirit the message of wisdom, to another the message of knowledge by means of the same Spirit, to another faith by the same Spirit, to another gifts of healing by that one Spirit, to another miraculous powers, to another prophecy, to another distinguishing between spirits, to another speaking in different kinds of tongues, and to still another the interpretation of tongues. All these are the work of one and the same Spirit, and he gives them to each one, just as he determines.

—1 CORINTHIANS 12:1–11

I taught directly from Scripture; then I also related what I had learned from Lance Pittluck on the telephone several weeks earlier. On this night I had changed the order of the service so that I taught first, then had praise and worship, and ended by inviting those present to share testimonies. When I gave the invitation for testimonies, someone stood at the back of the church and said, "Brother Randy, I think I'm having one of them there things you was just talking about 'cause there's nothin' wrong with my right wrist, but it's killin' me!" And there I stood, thinking, *Oh no! What have I gotten myself into? I've really opened up Pandora's box this time; this poor woman must be suffering from the power of suggestion!*

I decided to wait and see if anyone responded before I judged the word of knowledge to be nothing more than that—the power of suggestion. When no one seemed to have a wrist problem, I passed the situation off as lightly as I could and sat down. We continued with business as usual for the remainder of the service. But right before the benediction, my best friend's wife, Barbara Gooch, stood up to address the congregation.

46

With tears streaming down her face, she said, "I've had pain in my wrists for years, and I can barely do any of the work that I should be doing. I've got three little kids, and I can't knit. I can't hold things for very long before my wrists are just killing me. I've had surgery on them twice, and I've had these plastic pieces inserted into them. But they still hurt. I don't want to have surgery again!"

The assistant pastor, a volunteer, and another deacon rose to their feet, and one of them said, "I knew that word was for Barb!" As we prayed for her wrists, Barbara Gooch received her healing. So much for the power of suggestion.[1]

NEXT COURSE: DREAMS AND VISIONS

In January 1984 two of my deacons, Tom Simpson and Don Eldridge, and I found ourselves in Dallas, Texas, to attend James Robison's Bible Conference. The speakers included Paul (now David) Yonggi Cho, Peter Lord, David Wilkerson, Jim Hilton, James Robison, Dudley Hall, and John Wimber.

Until then I had experienced only one dream in my life that I could absolutely attribute to God. So what the Holy Spirit had in store for me next really got my attention. The night before the conference I had a dream that I have never been able to forget. In the dream I was standing before a man who was standing behind a wrought iron fence. About four feet above the ground there was a wall, and on the wall there was a commandment. It was not one of the Ten Commandments; nevertheless, I knew it was a commandment to me, and it was there to challenge me as to whether or not I would choose to obey it. I studied the commandment for a moment, and then I looked up at the man and said, "Yes, I'll obey."

He opened the gate, and I went up to the next level. When I got to the next level, I saw another wall that had not previously been visible to me. On it another commandment was written. This time it involved a test; I was commanded to do something. The man said to me, "Will you obey this?"

I answered, "Yes," and he opened the second gate as well.

I stepped up onto the next tier and saw another wall, where another commandment had been written. At this point the dream ended.

I knew the dream was from God. But what was I to do with it?

As I pondered the dream, I began to realize that it had been given to me as a word for both me and my church. I knew that the Lord wanted to take us higher, into a closer relationship with Him, and that He wanted to take us up into a higher realm of the Spirit. From the dream I could also see that with each progression there would be a higher level of accountability. At each level there would be things in my own life that would have to be surrendered to God continually.

The next day I arrived at the conference over an hour early and stood in line. John Wimber would be teaching the pastors that day, and this session would be attended by only about five hundred people as opposed to the general session, which would probably draw a crowd of at least eight thousand. I wanted to get there early so I could get a seat on the first row. I wanted to be close enough to be able to see everything—tears, facial expressions during the conviction of the Holy Spirit—everything!

John Wimber came to the platform and began to teach, and I was absolutely blown away. He had words of knowledge for those who were present, and I loved what he was saying. I was captivated. As he began to pray for a woman who had been called forward to receive a word of knowledge, Wimber said, "Now watch her. See what the Holy Spirit is doing!"

As my deacons and I watched from the front row, we could see that the hem of her dress had begun to shake!

I nudged Tom and Don and said, "Hey, did you see that? Her dress is shaking!"

I was really excited because I had never seen anyone have a physical reaction to the Holy Spirit other than being under obvious conviction. All of this was entirely new to me. Then the woman began to shake even more profoundly. She touched someone else, and that person began to shake also.

During John Wimber's time of teaching and ministry, people

were also getting healed. We were learning many new things, and it was a wonderful experience.

FILLED WITH THE HOLY SPIRIT

Then David Yonggi Cho spoke, and God used the message of this great man of God to convict me of my need for more intimacy with God through a greater understanding of the Holy Spirit. When the meeting concluded I kept to myself for the rest of the afternoon because the Lord was dealing with my heart; I wanted to be alone with Him. I returned to the meeting that evening and heard David Wilkerson talk about the power of repentance. At the end of his ministry time, pastors came forward and fell on their faces in repentance, crying out to God.

Trinity Broadcasting Network's TV cameras were there, televising the conference. I knew the broadcast would be seen back home. In my pride, I didn't want to kneel or put my face on the ground because I feared that if my friends and congregation saw me, they might lose confidence in my ability to lead them. But everybody around me was weeping, and all I could think was, *Man, this is being beamed back to Marion, Illinois, and they're going to see me!*

I knew such fear resulted from pride, and finally I knelt down and prayed. Then I stood up and began to sing. I felt that the Holy Spirit was telling me, "Raise your hands!" But I was a Baptist, and Baptists didn't do that. Nevertheless, I was beginning to know the voice of the Holy Spirit more clearly so I raised my hands. As soon as I did, the Spirit of God hit me, and I knew that I was about to lose it emotionally. I looked around me and saw a large projection screen. I headed for it because I thought I could get behind it and hide. But as I neared it, the Spirit of God hit me again, and I fell against a wall, slid down it, and wound up sprawled on the floor—visible to everyone. I lay there shaking and crying for nearly half an hour.

As I got up to return to my chair, the Spirit hit me again, and I slid back down the same wall into a heap on the floor where I lay weeping and shaking some more.

One of my deacons told me later that they had been looking for me. Finally one of them pointed up to the front of the auditorium, where both men saw me lying beneath that projection screen in front of all eight thousand people.

MY FIRST ENCOUNTER WITH JOHN WIMBER

The next night I approached John Wimber, following his ministry time, and introduced myself. Then I said, "John, I'm not worthy enough for you to pray for me, but would you pray for a couple of my deacons?"

As I turned to motion Tom and Don to come forward, Wimber caught both my hands and said, "No, I want to pray for *you!*" As he looked deeply into my eyes, I knew he was receiving words of knowledge about me. I was afraid he would see every one of my imperfections and even some of my pain. I felt so exposed and expected the worst to come out of his mouth.

Wimber said, "I want to pray for you; but first I want to pray for your heart because you've been wounded lately in your church."

It was true. Only a few months earlier I had experienced some fresh wounds that had not yet had time to heal, so I knew his word was from the Lord. He spoke to me about several things.

"You're a prince in the kingdom of God," he said. Now I didn't quite know what to do with that. Then he said, "There's an apostolic call on your life." I didn't learn until ten years later in 1994 that when John used that term he meant that I would one day wind up having a translocal ministry. He shared many good prophecies with me as he prayed, and I went away very encouraged.

GOD'S POWER HITS HOME

Just a few weeks later, March rolled around and it was time for the healing conference at my own church. I was excited about the team John Wimber had sent to us, which included Blaine Cook.[2]

The first afternoon Blaine Cook taught on spiritual gifts and held a "clinic" where he called out words of knowledge. Some of the people who came forward for prayer fell down under the power of the Spirit. Many people in my church, including Sandy, the pianist, had never seen God's power come in this manner and were quite uneasy with it. They were literally trying to get away. Sandy had made it to the back of the church and was ready to leave when the Vineyard team prayed for her and she too was slain in the Spirit.

Though many other people were slain in the Spirit, I felt nothing. I told my friend Tommy Gooch, "You know, I feel like a kid who's got the flu and has to stay inside the house and look out the picture window watching everybody else play. I'm just watching and nothing's happening to me." I really wanted to be touched by God.

We made it through the afternoon session of the first day and came to the evening session. I sat in the front row. As we approached the ministry time Blaine said, "The Holy Spirit's on the front row. He is moving on people in the front row." We had three front rows, and I didn't feel anything, so I assumed it had to be one of the other two. Then Blaine said, "Randy, the Spirit of God is on you." I've found out since then that some people can be so dense and dull to the Holy Spirit that other people can see the Spirit on them before they can actually sense it themselves. I was one of those dense and dull ones!

GOD'S POWER HITS *ME!*

Blaine said, "Randy, just hold your hands up." Now, I was on the front row, and this was my church—my Baptist church. We just didn't hold our hands up, but I decided to go for it anyway. As soon as I started to raise my hands, I felt a giant vacuum sweeper in the sky suck them all the way up. Then it felt as if I were hooked into an electric fence. I was shaking from the top of my head to the bottom of my feet. I was shifting my weight from one foot to the other trying to keep from falling to the floor.

Then I heard Blaine call out, "DeAnne, the Spirit of God's on you." I heard my wife crying, and I wanted to watch, but I was frozen in position. I couldn't turn my head to see her. Down she went. (Later she told me that she felt as if a whole bunch of people were pushing on her, but in reality no one even touched her.) She also felt a heat in her chest, which later proved to be an emotional healing from tormenting memories of her father's death.

After the service that night, while we were lying in bed, I asked DeAnne, "What did you think of the service tonight?" She answered, "Well, it was all right, but I don't think that has to happen every time!"

I had no way of knowing it then, but major changes were just ahead as the Lord took DeAnne and me on a roller-coaster adventure, filled with quick changes and many wonderful manifestations of His miraculous provision. And, just as John Wimber had prophesied, the journey would eventually take me all around the world.

FOUR

PRUNING

I am the true vine, and My Father is the vinedresser. Every branch in Me that does not bear fruit He takes away; and every branch that bears fruit He prunes, that it may bear more fruit.

—JOHN 15:1–2, NKJV

GOD TAKES US through pruning seasons from time to time, removing the dry, dead branches so even more growth can take place, which in turn will produce a bumper crop of fruit unlike anything we have ever experienced. DeAnne's and my "pruning season" began almost immediately after the Vineyard's healing conference ended.

Many of us were powerfully impacted by what we had learned during the healing conference, and I could sense that God had many changes in store for us as we continued to seek His perfect will for our lives.

Things were different since the conference—that much I

could definitely determine. For one thing, John Gordon had begun to move out powerfully in the gift of healing. For another, the power of God had seemed to intensify among us.

On one occasion shortly after the conference, as John Gordon and I prayed for a woman's wrists to be healed, DeAnne (as usual!) "fell out" in the Spirit. I glanced over at DeAnne and got tickled because she'd fallen on the floor again. *What's new?* I thought. Only this time, there *was* something new: DeAnne complained that she could not get up. To that, John's wife, Margie, replied, "That's okay, honey! Just lie right there and enjoy it!" It was the first time any of us had seen someone stuck to the floor, unable to get up—and to think that it had happened to my very own, once-skeptic wife!

There were other changes, too. For instance, we had suddenly become aware of the demonic realm. One of the conference sessions had been on the topic of deliverance and the healing of the demonized. The Vineyard people told us, "You are just getting started, so we don't want to spend a lot of time on this. We don't want you to run around thinking you have demons under every rock. Don't even deal with the subject of demons unless you have one talking to you. You're going to need some more training on deliverance, and we don't have time to do it in these meetings."

And there was yet another change: I had discovered that I wanted to join the Vineyard movement.

"BUT WE'RE BAPTISTS!"

I told DeAnne that on the way home from church right after the conference ended. "But we're Baptists!" she responded, as I had fully believed she would. "We don't know anything about the Vineyard!"

"I know," I assured her. "But I agree with everything I've seen and heard so far. I believe in the values they espouse, in their style of ministry, their style of worship, the way they pray for healing—everything. And everything I've learned about these guys tells me that this is what I've been waiting for my whole life."

I could tell that it scared DeAnne to hear me talk like this, so I dropped the subject of joining the Vineyard. We didn't talk much more about it . . . for awhile at least.

In the meantime, things were happening right there at Spillertown Baptist Church. My assistant pastor, who had been slain in the Spirit at the healing conference, had received his prayer language and now prayed in tongues. His wife, the assistant Sunday school superintendent, had had a similar experience. She too had received a prayer language. Eight other church members had received their prayer languages. Twenty others had fallen under the power of God, and many of those had come forward with shaking hands, as evidence that they had been anointed by God to pray for the sick. Yes, the healing conference had been quite an experience for us all. Manifestations of the power of God were now occurring regularly in our midst.

In a matter of weeks, we had witnessed our first demonic manifestation.

One night as I prayed for John Gordon's business, a woman standing nearby was suddenly thrown backward. It was as if someone had doubled up a fist and hit her in the face, knocking her down. She landed at least six feet from where she had been standing. Now this totally shocked me because I had no idea what was going on. As this woman lay on the floor, John and I walked over to her to check this thing out. As we looked down at her, her eyes flew open, and both eyes were rolling in opposite directions. As one eye rolled to the top, looking out at right angles, the other eye was clear at the bottom, pointing left. Her face appeared to be incredibly distorted, and her neck and forehead were swollen with what seemed to be fluid. As she prayed in tongues her tone of voice seemed mean and angry. Eventually she closed her eyes and calmed down, and I thought, *I'm glad that's over with!*

Only it wasn't. John whispered in my ear, "You know what we have here, don't you?"

I just looked at him and replied, "John, don't say that! We don't have one talking to us, and we're not going to get involved unless we do. *There's nothing talking to us!*"

All of a sudden the woman started flip-flopping on the floor and making screaming sounds. As she bounced around, her eyes flew open and started their out-of-sequence rotation once more. Just then she fixed her eyes on John and said, in the loud, deep voice of a man, "I hate you! You're ugly!"

John and I exchanged looks, and I said, "Okay, *now* we've got one talking to us!"

We had no idea what to do with the demonic display on the floor before us. So we commanded the demon to come out in the name of Jesus. We yelled at it, screamed at it, made the sign of the cross over the woman, put an actual cross on her, and finally smeared anointing oil on her—anywhere we thought it was needed. We tried to threaten the demon and told it we were going to ask God to torture it in hell if it didn't come out. We tried everything to get it to come out of her.

Finally I remembered that Blaine Cook, who led the team from the Vineyard, had mentioned that his wife was anointed and trained in the area of deliverance. I told one of the deacons, "Call her!" Unbelievably, the phone lines at the church were dead. So I left John in charge and ran next door to the educational building to phone Becky Cook in California for a long-distance crash course in deliverance prayer. Again the phone lines were dead. I sent a woman to her house to call Becky.

Becky Cook walked the believer through the biblical procedure for casting out a demon. She returned to the sanctuary where the woman was still writhing on the floor under demonic influence. The woman who had been receiving instructions from Becky Cook returned with a page of notes in her hand, which she proceeded to read to us as we prayed:

"Step one, blah-blah-blah. . . . "

GOD TEACHES US ABOUT DELIVERANCE

It sure sounds funny now, but the Lord honored our efforts, even though none of us knew what we were doing. The demon departed; the woman was delivered; and we were suddenly in the business of casting out demons.

Prior to that night, I had refused to believe that demons were real. I thought demonic possession was psychosomatic and that demons were mythological. I was even certain that the instances in which Jesus had dealt with demonic possession had merely been His own way of simply condescending to the ignorance-based views of first-century man. But any doubts I ever had about the reality of demons or demonic activity ended that night—for me, at least.

That first deliverance session lasted until three o'clock in the morning. Afterward we were all worn out, but we knew none of us could leave until the woman had been filled with the Holy Spirit.

We knew about the biblical warning that a house swept clean could be inhabited by seven demons worse than the first if it were not first properly filled. That passage of text from Luke states:

> When an unclean spirit goes out of a man, he goes through dry places, seeking rest; and finding none, he says, "I will return to my house from which I came." And when he comes, he finds it swept and put in order. Then he goes and takes with him seven other spirits more wicked than himself, and they enter and dwell there; and the last state of that man is worse than the first.
>
> —LUKE 11:24–26, NKJV

I realized the people of Spillertown Baptist needed some teaching on the subject of spiritual authority—and soon, before there were to be any more episodes such as the first one. So the following Sunday I taught on Colossians 2:13–15, emphasizing verse 15: "And having disarmed the powers and authorities, he [Jesus] made a public spectacle of them, triumphing over them by the cross."

After I taught, I gave an invitation for those who wanted to be saved or rededicate their lives to Christ to come forward. I also invited those forward who wanted prayer for healing. There at the front was the woman we had prayed for until 3:00 A.M. I waited to pray for her last.

57

DRUNK IN THE SPIRIT

After the altar ministry was completed, the ministry team and I stayed behind to pray for this woman. This time eight demons were cast out of her, but the deliverance went smoothly and didn't take as long. We felt as though this time we knew what we were doing and made quick business of casting out the demons. As she was gloriously empowered by the Holy Spirit, so overwhelmed by the Spirit was she that she was laughing and staggering, unable to walk without help from her husband. She appeared to be drunk—just as the Book of Acts has mentioned. That was in 1984, and to this day she has not had further trouble with demonization.[1]

God used this and other real-life experiences to teach me and my ministry team about the reality of demons and how to pray effectively for the demonized. One of the most profound examples was that of Mary (not her real name). One afternoon John Gordon and I led deliverance prayer for this thirty-nine-year-old woman who had been suffering for many years from grand mal epileptic seizures. Mary was losing her vision, had severe arthritis, and was already walking with a walker, bent over and forced to take small, painful steps much the same as a very old woman would walk. We explained to her that we would pray for her and command the demons afflicting her to cease and come out; while we did not plan to yell at her or to hit her, if we did raise our voices, she should not interpret that as being aimed at her but at the demonic forces against which we would be directing our prayers. But before praying for her we wanted to pray to God.

As soon as we started to pray, Mary fell out of her chair. I panicked, but John seemed very composed. He walked over to her, pointed his finger at her, and commanded, "You spirit of fire, come out of her!" As I was wondering, *What in the world is going on?*, he added, "You spirit of wind, come out of her!" Mary had begun to scream and spit.

We have finally gone off the deep end, I thought. *John has lost it.*

John kept right on praying: "I know all about you! You tried to kill me last night! You tried to strangle me in my sleep, and I even know your name!" The next thing he did was name a particular town and said, "What about that?"

At the mention of the town, Mary really went nuts—spitting, clawing, and screaming. John kept right on pressing, "And what about Mike?" Again, Mary was reacting in an extreme manner, while I had absolutely no idea what to make of what I was observing. Then John said, "And what about adultery?"

Mary had another violent reaction and started to scream, "No! I didn't do it! I didn't do it!"

John said, "Yes, you did! God showed me! He told me!"

To that, she cried out, "No, I did not! I did not! I caught him in the act of adultery—in the garage, with a sixteen-year-old girl!"

Then John backed up and said, "I'm sorry! God didn't say it was you; He just spoke the word *adultery.*"

Her cousin, who was present with us in the room, pulled John aside and asked, "How did you know about all this? She has never told anyone except her mother and me."

"The Lord showed me," John explained. "He gave me a full-blown vision."

It turned out that Mary had been raped by a man named Mike in the town John had named when she was just sixteen. When she told her mother about it, her mother ordered, "Don't ever tell anyone about that!" So she had stuffed it down for twenty-three years.

It also turned out that her grandfather had been a Cherokee medicine man. He had taken her down into a cave where there were snakes and said, "The spirit of fire and the spirit of the wind will protect you." She had been forced to walk over hot coals and had been deeply demonized as a result.

These spirits of fire and wind were the ones identified to John by the Holy Spirit—the ones we had cast out of her in prayer.

I was amazed because I had never seen the word of knowledge operating with such precise accuracy. John later explained to me that in the middle of the previous night, evil spirits had awakened him and tried to strangle him as he wrestled against them in prayer. In fear of the evil presence, John said he called out to Jesus, the spirits left immediately, and God gave him the vision revealing the root cause of the woman's demonization.[2]

Once the deliverance was over, I prayed for Mary that the Lord would heal her of all past hurts. We spent some time praying more generally for her. At the end of several hours Mary walked out minus her walker; she has never had another grand mal seizure.[2]

WE JOIN THE VINEYARD

I had been struggling for months with a decision I knew I could no longer postpone: I believed I had to join the Vineyard. I even talked with some of the Vineyard's leaders to determine whether my church could remain American Baptist and also be duly aligned with the Vineyard at the same time. They encouraged me to stay in the Baptist denomination as long as I could, while also confiding in me what I already knew—that my days as a Baptist were numbered. "You're already one of us," they assured me. "You've got our values."

So during a twenty-day fast I asked God for more precise direction regarding what I should do about joining the Vineyard. "Am I supposed to leave the Baptist church and join the Vineyard, or what?" God told me to end the fast and to celebrate my wedding anniversary.

The next day the matter was taken out of my hands. It all started to unwind the night DeAnne and I were interviewed on WTCT, the local TBN affiliate. During the course of the program, we related what God had been doing at Spillertown Baptist Church. After the program, as DeAnne and I returned to the church, one of the trustees approached our car and tried to drag me out from behind the wheel. He was absolutely livid with me for going on TV and telling everyone what the Holy Spirit had been doing in our midst. I recalled a very odd conversation DeAnne and I had had earlier that same evening: "DeAnne," I had asked her, "do you realize that all it takes to have a vote of confidence to have me fired is ten signatures on a petition?"

That remark had been prophetic in nature—just such a petition had already been mounted and was circulating within the church. The petition led to a vote of confidence, which—surprisingly— I won. But by then I felt that the Lord had told me that I was to leave Spillertown Baptist Church and become part of the Vineyard. Even though the vote of confidence had shown that a full 80 percent of the congregation had voted for me, in September 1984 I resigned.

And I had absolutely no idea what to do next.

A few people left the church with me and asked, "Randy, will you pastor us? We have been told by the violent minority that since we believe the way you do, we should leave with you."

So DeAnne and I and about twenty others started a Vineyard church in Southern Illinois. I never really intended to plant that church. I told the others that they had simply followed me out on the limb before I sawed it off. I promised to pastor them until I knew what I was supposed to do next. One thing I did know was that I was not supposed to stay in a small town, but to go to a city. I just didn't know which one.

LEARNING TO TRUST GOD

There I was, pastor of a small Vineyard congregation that within months had grown to seventy people. I was still waiting on God in prayer as to what to do next, since I still did not believe this was it. One Sunday during praise and worship I received a strong impression to ask the church to cut my salary by two thousand dollars. As I knew for certain that this thought could not have come from me, I figured it must have come from God. So I took it to DeAnne for confirmation. "Just tell the leadership after worship," she said.

So, after worship, I stood and said, "You know, I feel that the Lord just said you are supposed to cut my salary by two thousand dollars, and DeAnne and I want you to do that."

That was the first indication to me that the Lord was taking DeAnne and me on a journey to develop our faith and trust in Him. While the journey was difficult and fraught with problems, it would also prove to be exciting as God delivered us out of the midst of one crisis after another—with plenty of miracle answers to prayer in between. . . .

In January 1985 five of us packed into a '64 Chevy and drove to Dallas to attend James Robison's Bible Conference. We shared a single motel room each night. None of us had much money, and things were really tight. I had just taken that cut in pay, and we were really starting to feel it. But the day before we left for Dallas, John Gordon called me. He said, "Randy, I see you are going to St. Louis to start something there."

"Why did you say that?" I asked.

"Oh, I don't know; it just flew out of my mouth."

John had no way of knowing that I had been thinking about that very thing.

John Wimber had also called prior to the conference and had asked to meet with me while in Dallas.

But on the way to meet with John, I encountered David Thompson, a fellow I had once prayed for in Little Rock, Arkansas.

"Hey, are you going to the Signs and Wonders Conference out in Anaheim?" he asked.

"I don't have the money," I responded.

As we talked, Dave brought me up to date as to what the Holy Spirit had been doing in his life, and upon parting he said a curious thing to me: "See you in Anaheim."

Again I said, "Dave, I don't have the money; there's no way I can go out there."

"I will see you next month in Anaheim!" Dave insisted.

But I just laughed, shook my head, and held my ground: "I don't think so!" And I went on to my meeting with John Wimber.

While I was with John, he also asked me if I would be coming to the conference. "I'd like to attend," I admitted, "but we really can't afford it."

"How much would it cost to fly you out?"

"A little over seven hundred dollars," I responded, in complete shock.

"Well, I want you to come, so I'll send you a check."

Well, that's wonderful, I thought. *But what am I going to do about a motel, food, and transportation once I get out there?*

What I didn't quite realize yet was that DeAnne and I had entered an incredible season of our lives in which the Holy Spirit was beginning to teach us to trust God more than ever before for His miraculous provision to meet our needs in powerful new ways.

THE LORD MOVES IN MYSTERIOUS WAYS

While we were still out in Dallas, John Wimber had introduced me to another couple. This couple had never heard our conversation about the conference or about my financial need. In fact, they knew nothing about me except my name. The man, Cliff, had just resigned his business and was wondering whether he should join the Vineyard. As he and his wife and I talked for the next half hour, the couple excused themselves for a brief private conference just before we parted. Cliff returned to me and said, "This has never happened to us before, but I really trust my wife's judgment, and she believes the Holy Spirit told her to give you a check for a thousand dollars. We want you to have it to attend training conferences this coming year."

I took it gratefully and added it to our church's conference fund. I was really excited, and from time to time I found myself shouting, "Thank You, God!", as I walked about Dallas. I didn't care who overheard me. Prior to that point in my ministry I had never received a contribution larger than twenty dollars. Now I had been given a check for a thousand dollars by a couple I barely knew.

But that same night after the service a fellow named Richard approached me and asked me if I would go out for steak and eggs with him—his treat! I had only enough money for a hamburger, so that really sounded good to me. I agreed to go, and while we were driving in his van to the restaurant, I excitedly told him about the thousand-dollar gift I had received earlier in the day. When we arrived at the restaurant, the man told his wife, "Honey, you go on in; I want to sit here a minute and talk to Randy."

Then he said, "The reason I wanted to talk to you is that when I first saw you yesterday the Holy Spirit told me I was to write you a check for a thousand dollars." I was speechless! He had planned to send me a check for that amount when I got home but instead gave it to me. He added that he did not want the money to go to the church; he said he wanted me to keep it for my personal needs.

As I told DeAnne about the two checks, she was overjoyed. "That's really interesting, Randy," she said, "because we just got a bill yesterday for one thousand forty dollars for the interest payment on the car." As we only had forty dollars in the bank the day before, this was indeed perfect timing. Then she said as an afterthought, "Oh, by the way, Edna Brown called!"

Edna Brown, an African-American Baptist pastor from St. Louis, was someone I trusted implicitly. "What did Edna have to say?" I inquired.

"She said that you are to go to St. Louis and start a work there."

It was just the confirmation I had needed.

In one twenty-four-hour period God had provided me with two thousand dollars and had confirmed that He was indeed leading me to St. Louis. I went directly home from Dallas to put the house up for sale.

BUT ALL WAS NOT ROSES . . .

I had hoped that my congregation in Marion, Illinois, would be happy for us that we had heard from God about our good fortune and our approaching move to St. Louis. Instead of sharing our joy, they felt rejected. And because we had told them about the two thousand-dollar gifts, they stopped giving. We were soon in serious financial trouble.

In August DeAnne and I went to a conference in San Diego that John Wimber had again paid for us to attend because I was invited to teach one of the workshops. Things were really tight, and on the way to the conference I told DeAnne that I had decided to get a secular job to get us through. We had also decided that we would not mention our need within the Christian community; we wanted God's sovereign intervention in our circumstances, not charity.

We wanted to see His provision, so we agreed that we would only tell the Lord of our financial needs.

When we arrived in San Diego, the first person we ran into was Dave Thompson. "How are you doing?" he asked.

"I'm doing all right," I said, "But I'm going to have to take a job for awhile."

"Doing what?"

"I don't know."

"I'll give you a job," he offered.

"Doing what?"

"Training people to fry donuts."

"I don't know how to fry donuts, much less teach others to fry them," I said and laughed.

"I know; we'll train you first."

He promised that all I would have to do was fry some donuts and let the trainees watch. Then I was to let them fry as I watched. I thought this was significant, because this was the same method used by the Vineyard leaders to train their people. So I said, "I can do that."

One problem solved. And God was about to solve another—a very large one.

A man I had previously met approached me and said, "I'm going to be real blunt. God has told me that you have a need and that I am supposed to meet it. How much do you need?"

Now I could have said I needed hundreds when he only planned to give me twenty; or I could say twenty when he had planned to give me hundreds. So I simply stated, "Well, if God has told you to help me, why don't you ask Him how much you are supposed to give me?"

"No, it's not supposed to be that way," he said. "You have to tell me what you need."

I then explained to him that DeAnne and I had purchased a new Buick Park Avenue when things were going well and that we had had plenty of cash before we left Spillertown.

But then everything changed once we were empowered by the Spirit. DeAnne quit her job; I resigned my pastorate; and we were behind in our bills so that the car had become a financial noose around our necks. I had put so many miles on it driving back and forth to conferences that we would have to take a beating if we tried to sell it. I still needed a big car because I was taking a carload of people with me to every conference.

I was about to ask, "Can you help me with a car payment that I have fallen behind on?" But before I could, this man asked, "How much do you owe on that car?"

"Seven thousand," I replied.

The man looked at his wife and told her, "Write him a check for seven thousand dollars."

"Whoa, wait a minute!" I said, in shock over the man's generous gesture. "That's a lot of money! That's seven thousand dollars! You can't do that!"

"Yes, this is God!" the man and his wife insisted. And while the woman wrote out the check, the man opened his wallet and counted out five one-hundred-dollar bills. "You're going to need this when you get home," he said.

Once again I was blown away by what God was doing. What I had forgotten was that not only did we owe seven thousand on the car; we also owed five hundred and twenty dollars more in accumulated interest.

What a testimony we were able to give to the men in the loan department at the bank when DeAnne and I arrived, cash in hand, to pay off our car!

THE HANDWRITING ON THE WALL

Our church membership seemed to react negatively to our having received another mysterious cash gift. The offerings grew even worse. I was beginning to believe that God was allowing this to happen because DeAnne still did not want to go to St. Louis. She wanted to stay in Marion where all her friends were. I knew it was God's plan to wean us from the place we knew; this time He was using hardships to prepare DeAnne to be willing to go on.

In a few weeks we were once again in serious financial trouble, receiving little or no money from the church. DeAnne said to me, "Randy, I don't think anybody loves us; I'm not even sure God loves us."

That's what the pressure was doing to her. She was so discouraged that I was not able to console her. On top of all our usual bills, we also owed one thousand dollars for our life and health insurance, as well as a payment for our car and homeowner's insurances. All the bills were due at once, and we didn't have the money.

That same day the mail contained a check for a thousand dollars and a note that read, "I just wanted you to know that I love you, and God loves you guys."

I ran to show the check and note to DeAnne; she broke down and cried when she read it. God had once more evidenced to us that He loved us and that we were in His plan. The timing of this note was a powerful witness to us regarding both God's ability to provide for us and of His loving care for us as His children.

LESSONS IN THE MIDDLE OF THE STORMS

As the financial storms raged about us, it was unmistakable that DeAnne and I were learning about God in powerful new ways. As He pruned us and poured more of His Spirit into us, it seemed for a time that we were producing hardly any fruit for His kingdom. But we were learning much about it.

We learned, for instance, that Matthew 6:33 is true: "But seek first his kingdom and his righteousness, and all these things will be given to you as well." Again and again DeAnne and I had seen God perform the miraculous in terms of His sovereign provision, and we were grateful. I believe that during this period of our lives God also taught us the secret of Philippians 4:12—"the secret of being content in any and every situation." These were, in fact, the glory years . . . soon to be followed by the desert years when there was even less fruit to show for our all-out efforts to minister in the power of the Holy Spirit.

In 1983 we had made forty-two thousand dollars. Now our income had dropped to next to nothing. That's hard to take. It got so bad that we had to cash in our IRA, which meant that we incurred heavy penalties. Now the IRS was hounding us to collect fifteen hundred dollars in income and social security taxes. Again God provided fourteen hundred eighty dollars through two couples who knew nothing of our need. This occurred at the conference where I consented to take the job frying donuts.

I thought God would not be in it, but He was. . . .

✺ FIVE ✺

POWER

But you will receive power when the Holy Spirit comes on you;
and you will be my witnesses in Jerusalem, and in all Judea
and Samaria, and to the ends of the earth.

—ACTS 1:8

DEANNE AND I have learned the hard way that God's system of promotion is a whole lot different from man's. Man's way of getting promoted is to work hard, learn the system, then use that same system to get ahead. Man's way relies on contacts and favors and "who you know." Man's way relies on plenty of elbow grease and even a thing called "luck." Man works hard for his promotion, and after he gets it, he likes to take the credit for all the grueling effort he put into it. That's what I have come to call the "performance mentality."

But God's way of promoting is far different. He delights in exalting the humble person who has elected to take the lower seat in the event that he will some day—for reasons only known to God Himself—be invited to come up higher. I like to call that method of promotion "going down to get up."

With an act of our will, we step down from our own agendas for our lives. Then, as we pray, we begin to pick up small, everyday insights into God's greater plans for us. We may not get it all at once; we may get only pieces of it now and then as God fits the small steps of our obedience together, crafting it into a beautiful tapestry that will one day be completely unfolded.

In the meantime, to everyone but God, it seems that we are just going backward . . . failing . . . and going nowhere fast.

When it seemed that all I was doing was frying dumb donuts on the 5:00 A.M. shift, in God's sight I was showing myself faithful in the small things so that when the time came, He could promote me. I would be ready. To everyone else, what I was doing in St. Louis looked like complete folly. But by now I had stepped too far away from that performance mentality to go back to it. I *couldn't* go back. My heart was just no longer in it.

So, as I fried those ridiculous donuts, I began to care more about what God was doing in my life than I cared about how it appeared outwardly to the rest of the world.

The performance mentality is practically unavoidable in Christians. It's impossible to overcome unless the power of God moves in to change our erroneous thinking that we must "do something" for God in order to "purchase" our position in His sight. *We may actually believe we're earning our place at God's table through our good works and outstanding effort on His behalf. How tragic!*

Performance mentality also tells us that it's possible to get ourselves "right enough" to be powerfully used by God. Contrary to the Scriptures that assure us "no one is good but One, that is, God" (Matt. 19:17, NKJV), and "I know that nothing good lives in me, that is, in my sinful nature" (Rom. 7:18), performance mentality deceives us into believing that we can work our way "good" enough for God to pour His Spirit out through us. We may even develop the mistaken idea that it is *we* who are the powerful ones, rather than the one God, who is all-powerful. In fact, His power must first move through our frail clay vessels and sanctify them in order for Him to use any of us! It took a while for me to learn that one—and I didn't learn it overnight.

I was once a perfect example of one who spent so much time and energy trying to please God and thereby earn His approval that I almost missed the free gift of His grace. His grace, I discovered, was being perfected daily in my weaknesses. And, as I fried donuts, I discovered that I had plenty of weaknesses.

Deep inside I really felt as if I were a failure. My failed first marriage had devastated me. Inside I sincerely believed the words that had been spoken over me by others in the Christian community: "You'll never have a ministry!" For ten long, arduous years, I had been in a season of intense spiritual preparation, but I still doubted whether God could or even *would* use me when the season was over. Could He really use someone like me—an ordinary man, a failure—to reach lost and hurting souls around the world?

As I came to know God more intimately, I also came to know myself; in fact, I knew right where my secret sins were located. I knew the attitudes and heart issues that I still struggled with, and as the Holy Spirit shined His light into these previously darkened areas of my soul, I more than ever saw myself as someone God might never be able to use—at least not powerfully or on a large scale. Yet inside me was this burning zeal for revival and evangelism; would I ever be released to follow that call?

During this important decade in my life the Lord built His values into me. It began at age thirty-one and ended when I turned forty. That decade was the greatest, and the most difficult, of my life.

While the best was yet to come, the Lord taught me the importance of relying totally on Him if I would ever be able to tap into the power of His spiritual gifts—power that too often remains entirely untapped in us. He taught me how much more can be accomplished in life and ministry once we set aside intellect and reason and the performance mentality, and begin to plug into His matchless ability to *perform for us*—"immeasurably more than all we ask or imagine" (Eph. 3:20).

Donuts

Every day the alarm would go off at 3:00 or 4:00 A.M., and I would rise and mutter, "Time to fry donuts!" That was a hard season for DeAnne and me. Five days a week we lived in a cheap motel room in St. Louis. Weekends we'd drive back home to Marion, because the company I worked for would only pick up the tab on the room for the nights I worked. For eleven months we lived that way, and, as time went on, we came to hate the arrangement. Part of why we hated it, I am convinced, is that God had by now turned our hearts totally away from Marion and toward St. Louis. We couldn't wait to get there. But our house in Marion had not yet sold, and I was putting hundreds of miles on the old Buick, driving to eighty stores in three states to train employees to fry a tasty donut.

This period was especially hard for me because I'm a night person. After working all day, I'd come home and set up meetings in the evening. DeAnne and I didn't know a soul in St. Louis. We were starting from scratch. I'd spend time building relationships with people in the hope that when I finally got to St. Louis they would come to the church I intended to start. It was also a difficult time for DeAnne because she was pregnant. The three-hundred-mile round trip each weekend was beginning to take its toll on her.

Our daughter, Johannah, was born July 26, 1986, and by Thanksgiving we finally moved into a house in St. Louis. The financial pressures had eased somewhat, but I was still making only about fifteen thousand dollars a year. During that time we survived by relying on assistance from food pantries and health care from public clinics. Our income remained low enough to continue to need such assistance for the next several years.

The St. Louis Church

John Wimber had warned me that starting a church from ground zero would not be easy; he was right. Now, eleven months into the work, DeAnne and I had only eleven people in our flock. I was still forced to fry donuts. One of the obstacles to church growth was the fact that we still didn't know many people in the St. Louis area. The other chief obstacle was that we had no praise and worship team—and anointed praise and worship had always been one of the hallmarks of a Vineyard church.

DeAnne and I listened to the beautiful recordings made in Anaheim, California, at the Vineyard there, and I would sigh, "Oh, if we could just have a worship team like that one!" We began to pray that God would send us musicians with a heart for Him. We prayed like that from January 1986 to Easter 1988, when God brought us two men who are now our worship leaders at the St. Louis Vineyard. Within a week of their arrival, we had started a worship team that was good enough to lead worship in a church of thousands.

I lost my job frying donuts after the company I had been working for was sold—and found myself back in full-time ministry. In order to minister full-time, I needed twelve hundred dollars a month. Our eleven-person congregation's monthly commitments totaled nine hundred. Still, DeAnne and I prayed about whether it was time to go back into full-time ministry, and the Lord said, "Do it!"

In confirmation that we had made the right choice, we again began to receive mysterious cash gifts. During the "donut years," we had not received one financial gift. Now the giving had resumed, which was a great encouragement to us.

GROWTH AND CHANGE

The church was growing, and we were now too large a congregation to meet in the school auditorium we had been renting for our services. That was the year the Lord provided two very large financial gifts in the amounts of sixteen thousand five hundred dollars and fifty thousand dollars. We raised another eighty thousand dollars and used the money to help us qualify for a loan to purchase the property we still occupy today. We moved into our new facility in January 1993.

The building had been in bankruptcy for six years before we

bought it. The systems were in terrible condition. The roof leaked. Soon we were physically worn out just trying to keep up with the necessary repairs. Yet, because we were faithful and refused to walk away from the responsibility, God turned it around. In the fall of 1993 the Lord changed the direction of the church.

I have often called the years between 1986 and 1993 "the desert years," because there were so many difficulties—both physically and spiritually. At Spillertown I had operated powerfully in the gifts of the Spirit and had seen signs and wonders as the fruit of my ministry. But I knew I had made none of those things happen—it was God who had poured His power out through me. None of those wonderful manifestations were happening now—and I was determined not to try to make something happen.

Outwardly it appeared that I was pastoring a powerless church when other Vineyards elsewhere appeared to be filled with manifestations of the power of the Holy Spirit.

This was hard for me to take. I knew I did not have control of the anointing. I often wondered why those earlier experiences of great power had diminished and why the healings and power encounters in the Holy Spirit were now so few and far between. As I shared these concerns with John Wimber, he gave me some wisdom that helped anchor me during the desert years. He said, "God's last orders are your standing orders until you get *new* orders!" So with those orders, I stood.

LESSONS IN THE DESERT

What had I learned during this very dry season? I learned so many things that it is difficult to count them all. Most of all, I learned the precious lesson of perseverance. Suddenly I understood what Paul wrote in Romans 5:3–5:

> Not only so, but we also rejoice in our sufferings, because we know that suffering produces perseverance; perseverance, character; and character, hope. And hope does not disappoint us, because God has poured out his love into our hearts by the Holy Spirit, whom he has given to us.

And now, because I had lived it for myself, I could understand what James wrote, in James 1:2–4:

> Consider it pure joy, my brothers, whenever you face trials of many kinds, because you know that the testing of your faith develops perseverance. Perseverance must finish its work so that you may be mature and complete, not lacking anything.

I learned the importance of being empowered by the Spirit regardless of whether there was much immediate fruit to show for it or little.

In fact, the most powerful experience I ever had with the raw power of the Holy Spirit occurred during the dry years. It happened at the 1989 regional meeting of the association of Vineyard churches, which was held at the Champaign Vineyard.

An Oasis in the Desert

During the final meeting (on October 27) I heard the Lord speak to me during the sermon, "You're for evangelism—you've always loved leading people to the Lord and preaching evangelistically." During the ministry time I went forward, hoping for a confirmation of that word. I received much more than that.

Words can only awkwardly describe my experience that night. As men of God prayed and prophesied over me, confirming my call to evangelism, the anointing of God resting on me grew more powerful. My right hand felt as if electricity were coursing through it. My left hand seemed to buzz with power. I overheard Ron Allen, who was praying for me, tell Happy Leman to "blow on my heart." That may sound like an odd thing to do, but when Happy puffed some air in my direction, I fell to the floor. At that moment my body felt as if it exploded with power.

On a scale of 0 to 10, with zero equaling no physical sensation as a witness to God's touch and 10 equaling a painful witness of power, I was at a 9 in both hands. I was thankful for what was happening, but I really was in pain. Groaning and weeping, I felt the electric sensation move throughout my body. My face felt as if electrical power were coursing through it, as if a lace fabric had been laid on my face and energized. My chest also seemed to be in an electric vice grip. Electrical sensations coursed through my entire body. I lost feeling in my hands and felt cramps in my feet.

When I first hit the floor I had stretched out with my hands over my head, but I ended up rolled over on my side in a fetal position. Through all of this, I was sweating from a feeling of intense heat.

Finally, the sensations subsided and I opened my eyes. During the experience I had felt no fear, but rather an awesome sense of the power, glory, and love of God. It was a turning point in my life.

Later I realized that God's touch had broken the power of a lurking, compulsive temptation that I had been very ashamed of. The Holy Spirit helped my face my fears and meet them head on with courage. But it was another four years before the gift of evangelism would begin to come forth. During that time I learned the importance of standing on God's last orders . . . until I got new ones.

SET ASIDE FOR LATER . . .

Often the Lord will set aside a believer for a period of preparation before he or she is released into actual ministry. That's what had been happening to me during this dry, desert period. It is during these critical, inactive, training periods that the Lord reveals His principles of ministry, thereby equipping the believer to step forth into the arena of ministry when the ground has finally been fully prepared.

Paul is an example of one who underwent this preparation process; after his powerful conversion experience on the road to Damascus, he was sent to Barnabas who prayed for him to receive his call into ministry. After that, he was trained in the things of God by the Holy Spirit and even produced fruit from a Roman prison.

Then there is the example of Jeremiah, whose years of wilderness preparation yielded a powerful prophetic ministry that warned the Israelites of impending Babylonian captivity and prepared a way of escape for some of the Jews—the prophet Daniel among them.

Joseph's years of hard preparation to lead Egypt and the Israelites through seven years of famine were spent in the dark, dank regions of Pharaoh's prison. In each case, God hid these individuals from public view and protected them from almost certain harm before releasing them into powerful ministry.

Even Jesus endured such a time of preparation. His first thirty years on earth were preparation for the brief three years of ministry that preceded His crucifixion and resurrection. But what a powerful three years! The signs and wonders produced during those three years were too numerous to list. The miracles of Jesus shook the world to its foundations—and the shaking continues yet today! So it is not so much the ministry that is responsible for producing much fruit, but the preparation process when the fruit seems small or when there may even seem to be no fruit at all.

Now I was coming into a new season. God was preparing me for release into ministry in a more powerful way than I had ever known. Strategic to releasing me into this new season of ministry was my attendance at a conference in Tulsa, Oklahoma, conducted by Rodney Howard-Browne, the South African evangelist responsible for bringing what charismatics were quick to term "the laughing revival." I didn't know what to make of it, so I went to see for myself. Forty-five hundred people were packed into the auditorium, and I watched as those around me appeared to be caught up in the proceedings, demonstrating various manifestations of joy and laughter. But there I sat for three sessions, completely unaffected.

I cringed inwardly when the evangelist announced, "Tomorrow morning I'll pray for everybody in the whole place!" I really didn't like the sound of that because I knew it would take too long. How many people do you think raised their hands when he asked who wanted prayer? You guessed it—all forty-five hundred! Now I was genuinely upset.

I had not gone there as a curiosity seeker. I had actually said to the Lord, "I don't want just to get touched. I want You to touch me in such a way that I can give Your power away and touch others!" As a matter of fact, I had even fasted prior to these meetings, and still I was getting nothing to speak of out of being there.

Please let me emphasize that I sincerely don't believe that fasting will get you any special "brownie points" with God. I don't think fasting will change His mind at all. What it does is cause us to focus on God, tuning out all the junk that ordinarily gets in the way.

I had been fasting for several weeks prior to these meetings and had gotten to the point where I was crying out, "Lord, I want to be touched by You so desperately that I'd grovel before You like an animal if that's what it's going to take! I'm not going to give up on You! I don't care what I have to do; I'm not going to eat until You touch me!" *That's* how hungry I was for God, and that's why I was so frustrated as I sat there, session after session, and everybody *but me* seemed to be receiving something wonderful from the ministry of Rodney Howard-Browne.

DESPERATE FOR A TOUCH FROM GOD

There's something about spiritual desperation that inevitably brings revival. God had put that sort of desperation in my heart. The flesh hates such desperation for God—only the Spirit can produce it. And only the Spirit can satisfy it.

So on that fourth and final morning of the Rodney Howard-Browne conference when he promised to pray for all forty-five hundred of us present, I got up from my place in the pew and got in line, just like everybody else. I even recall what I was thinking: *Okay, this is the last chance I have! I have to get all I can get!* I hate standing in line, even in restaurants. I don't want food badly enough to stand in line for it. Here I was, standing in line with forty-five hundred other people, waiting to get touched by God! It had to be God! As I stood there, the evangelist's voice boomed out over the PA system: "Fill! Fill! Fill!"

Finally, the evangelist stood in front of me, ready to pray. I thought, *Here he comes!* But instead of touching my shoulder, he slapped me gently on the head, and down I went. There I lay on the carpet, thinking, *Nothing happened! Again! This is not fair, God! What do I have to do? You know how hungry I am! I want to eat! What's it going to take? Why don't You just shake, rattle, and roll me? Let me feel that Holy Ghost electricity again, God!* But then I tried to get up from the floor, and I couldn't move. I was stuck to the floor. *Uh, oh! I don't feel any Holy Ghost electricity . . . but something's going on!*

SOMETHING'S GOING ON!

That's the first indication I had that God was doing something totally new on earth today. I lay on the floor for forty-five minutes while the evangelist walked around the auditorium, proclaiming, "Fill! Fill! Fill!" I didn't understand what was going on. I just thought, *This is my last chance,* and lay there until God was finished doing whatever it was that He was doing that I didn't understand.

At some point, I had taken my glasses off and put them in my pocket. When I could finally stand, I arose and went to another section of the auditorium and stood in another line (I still hated lines). When he came to me, Rodney Howard-Browne said, "You don't get drunk on a sip!" He slapped me on the head again, and again down I went. This time I was up and in another line before I knew it, and for a third time he slapped me as he prayed, "Fill! Fill! Fill!" This time I remember thinking, *Oh no! I'm in trouble now!* Down I went for a third time.

As I lay there on the soft carpet, I recalled what John Wimber had once told me: "You've got to learn to see what the Father is doing."

So for the rest of the morning I followed Rodney Howard-Browne all around the auditorium as he slapped people and proclaimed, "Fill! Fill! Fill!"

All the time I watched him, I was thinking, *What's he seeing? What's he hearing? What's he doing?* I had never seen anything like these meetings before. But I studied him intently as he ministered. I followed him around so closely that once an usher stopped me and asked, "Sir, can I help you?"

I answered, "No, I'm just seeing what God is doing. I'm trying to see what's going on here."

Finally, after different ushers had stopped me five or six times, the first usher came over to me again and said, "Look, you're going to have to quit because you're catching his eye, and it's bothering him."

"Okay," I said. "I respect authority. I was just watching. I don't want to bother him."

Since I couldn't follow Rodney Howard-Browne around anymore, I changed my focus to watching the results of his ministry. I prayed, *Lord, burn this into my mind so I'll never forget it.* I saw bodies everywhere—so many bodies laid out on the floor that the scene reminded me of the train station scene in *Gone With the Wind,* when wounded soldiers waiting for medical attention were laid out as far as the eye could see. That's what it looked like to me.

As I stood there observing the proceedings from a distance, Rodney Howard-Browne's brother, Basil, approached me and asked, "Sir, would you like to receive prayer?" I told him I had already been prayed for—three times! But this man who carries his own fivefold anointing answered, "That's all right! You look thirsty!" So I received prayer again.

It was at these meetings that God showed me how much His students loved Him. Because the meetings were hosted by the Faith camp I had attended while still harboring some mean-spirited attitudes toward the Faith people, I repented and asked God to forgive the harsh words I had spoken against the Faith camp, some even from the pulpit. While I still did not agree with all the doctrinal positions of the Faith camp, I realized just how precious all God's children were in His sight. And I became aware of just how displeased He was with the practice of attacking brothers and sisters. I went to a leader from Rhema Church and asked that person to forgive me for being mean-spirited against the church and its members.

On the way to the airport to catch our flight back home, my assistant pastor, Bill, said something to me that stopped me in my tracks: "Randy, I can hardly wait 'til we get home and this begins to happen at our church!"

"What did you say?" That seemed pretty unlikely, since I had been moving our church to the "seeker-sensitive" model. "Half the people there have hardly heard of the Holy Spirit!" I argued. "We have the liturgy, but we don't have the reality. When the reality comes, it's going to scare them to death! I need six months first just to teach them!"

But my assistant pastor said, "I can't wait that long!"

Finally, I got out my "big gun" and pulled rank on him. "I'm the senior pastor!"

Then God got out *His* big gun and pulled rank on *me*. The Holy Spirit spoke to my spirit and said: *"I'll do it when I want!"*

Humbly corrected, I turned to Bill and stated, "God will do it when He wants to, and I don't know when that is going to be!"

In my heart I believed I had at least six months until revival hit.

I was wrong.

GOD'S BOMB

Please understand that I had been pastor of this church in St. Louis for eight years, and in that entire time not one person had been slain in the Spirit. I preached the Sunday morning service following our trip to Tulsa, and the power of God hit us like a bomb. We began with teaching, followed by praise and worship, and right in the midst of praise and worship one of the backup singers went down, knocking a guitar stand over with a thud. She lay there, laughing and hitting her right thigh with her right hand. This went on for forty-five minutes of praise and worship.

She was a very sophisticated young woman from one of the wealthier families of our church, yet she lay on the floor laughing and slapping her thigh. When she arose later, she told us that right before she fell, she had seen the Shekinah glory cloud enter the church.

The power did not depart after praise and worship. I asked, "Would anyone like to receive ministry today?" Many came forward. This, in itself, was unusual. I had been accustomed to having very little response after such a prayer. On this day the altar was packed. As I prayed for the people at the altar, all I had to say was, "Bless you," and—boom!—down they went. We were going down the line, and the power of God was hitting, time after time, with people "laid out" in the Spirit. I was thinking, *This is wonderful! I can hardly believe it! Surely this must be a special circumstance!* But then the second service came, and the same thing happened. No one was more amazed than I was that day as God dropped the bomb.

Boom! Boom! Boom! Bodies lay everywhere around us as people "fell out" under the power of God. We were so excited at what God was doing that we invited people to come forward to give their testimonies. Everywhere we looked, people were laughing and having a great time. One girl came forward to take communion but fell out on the steps where I had planned to preach the next service. Later, during the testimonies, she began to laugh and shake, which disturbed my wife very much. DeAnne and I had been having a discussion for several weeks about what constituted order and what was out of order. The teenager's behavior upset DeAnne, and she said it made her nervous. I assured her that God was giving us an object lesson about what I was teaching—that God was, indeed, doing a brand new thing in our church.

SIGNS AND WONDERS FOLLOWING

Several weeks later was even better! At our Midwest regional meeting in Wisconsin, God showed up, and everybody got blasted! People were running and dancing, slapping each other, and generally acting drunk. Even Happy Leman (our regional overseer, whose nickname is "Mr. Control") was laughing hysterically! Anytime I see Happy that excited, I know it's got to be God!

Steve Phillips, my area pastoral coordinator, asked me to pray for him. Already drunk in the Spirit, he went down as I prayed for him. I just touched him, and the power of God hit him and knocked him into some chairs. He said it felt as if a truck had hit him. I didn't know that several years earlier he had had a spinal injury that caused him to awaken every morning in tears from intense pain. I had no way of knowing that his prognosis was not good and that he had been warned that it would be hopeless to try to correct the condition with surgery. But the power of God hit him and knocked him to the floor. As he lay there, he said it felt as if a hot hand had reached down into his stomach to pull something out. That night he was completely healed. The anointing of God was on him so strongly that he couldn't speak without stuttering for months afterward. Each time the Spirit of God would come upon him, he would stutter. In spite of this curious manifestation of the power of God, it was obvious to everyone who knew Steve that God had indeed done something wonderful for him.[1]

Word began to get around that God was moving powerfully in our midst, with signs and wonders following. One night after one of our meetings, I received a call from Pastor John Arnott of Toronto. He asked me to come to his church because he had heard about what happened at the regional meeting.

I recalled hearing Rodney Howard-Browne once say, "If you want to have revival, go north in the wintertime!"

If I hadn't heard that, I might never have gone to Toronto. After all, it was *January!* Still uncertain about what was happening in our midst in St. Louis, I decided to respond with caution.

"Why do you want me to come?" I asked.

"Because we've heard what just happened at your pastors' meeting."

"It might never happen again, John," I warned.

"I know," he admitted, "but I want you to come."

I asked if I could bring a team, and he said, "Yes." Then he told me he wanted me to preach four times.

"I can't preach four times! All I have is a testimony and one sermon!" But then I added, "I can bring my assistant, and he can preach to your kids and to the youth. We'll stay four nights, and then we'll come home. Okay?"

"That's fine," agreed John Arnott.

We had a deal. I was going to Toronto, and somehow John would get four meetings out of me. But I was nervous. Real nervous.

REVIVAL IN WINTER

Rodney Howard-Browne was right about winter and revival. It's a good incentive to keep moving when the temperature dips below zero, as it does in Toronto in January.

I was nervous, but not about the weather; I was worried that what had been happening in St. Louis was a fluke—that the power of God would not break out among us as we had experienced since my return from the Tulsa meetings conducted by Rodney Howard-Browne. Just the idea of another powerless meeting made me nervous.

But then I was encouraged by a vision given to Anni Shelton, my associate worship leader's wife. She told me she had seen a map of Toronto, and then she saw the city being set on fire. The blaze was moving out from Toronto all over the map. As she told me about the vision, she said, "I think God is going to start something in Toronto, and it's going to spread all over North America."

That vision may have encouraged me, but did it help my faith? No, it did not. When people would ask me, "Randy, what do you think is going to happen in Toronto?" I would respond lamely, "Well, I don't know—but I hope God shows up."

"YES, BUT WILL GOD SHOW UP?"

I don't know why it is, but I find myself comparing my heavenly Father with my earthly father—even though in my heart I know that there is really no comparison. From time to time I do it, even though I realize there is no point to it.

My earthly father had an eighth-grade education and did not work for a union. To keep his job, he sometimes had to work sixty to eighty hours a week in the oil fields of southern Illinois and Indiana. I didn't know him very well, but I knew he loved me.

Now I have a master of divinity degree, and I know my theology. I've had my Bible training, and yet what I knew in my head was very different from what I knew in my heart. In my heart I was comparing myself to great men of God like John

Wimber, Oral Roberts, and Billy Graham . . . and then there I was. I knew God would show up for one of them . . . but maybe not for me.

Probably not for me.

But my outlook changed as a result of a prophetic word given to me by Richard Holcomb the night before I left for Toronto.

THE PLACE OF PROPHECY

There's something else you need to know about me during this phase of my life and ministry: I didn't like prophecy. I thought it was too messy. I did not want my nice, neat, seeker-sensitive church contaminated by all the prophetic activity in the Kansas City Metro Vineyard, so I didn't encourage my people to go over there. And I certainly didn't want them coming over to my church. I did not place a very high value on the prophetic gifts. And to be perfectly honest, it had been some time since Richard and I had been in touch, so I was not aware that he had been prophesying to me for many years.

Each time he had a word for me, I simply assumed it was Richard and not God speaking because his words were so comforting, encouraging, and edifying. I never made the connection that Richard Holcomb was a prophetic voice in my life . . . until this particular night.

He said, "I have the second most clear word I have had for you since I met you, Randy."

"What is it?"

"The Lord says, 'Randy, test Me now. Test Me now. Test Me now! Do not be afraid. I will back you up! I want your eyes to be opened as Elisha prayed for Gehazi, that you will see into the heavenlies and see My resources for you. Do not become anxious because when you become anxious, you can't hear Me.'"

That prophetic word changed my life. It caused faith to rise up in me—faith to move in the anointing that I had received when Rodney prayed for me.

The next time someone asked me what it was that I thought God planned to do in Toronto, I said boldly: "We're getting ready to go on an apostolic mission out of the country, and we are going to see more of God than we have ever seen in our lifetime. God is going to show up!"

And He did. . . .

Six

TORONTO

*Do not remember the former things, nor consider the things of
old. Behold, I will do a new thing, now it shall spring forth.*
—ISAIAH 43:18–19, NKJV

G OD, IN FACT, did show up in Toronto—and in a powerful
and unmistakable way. The meetings that we had expected
to last four nights went on . . . and on. . . . I arrived in Toronto in
January 1994 and stayed, at the invitation of John Arnott, for
forty-two of the first sixty days of a revival that is still going on.
What began as a simple series of revival meetings developed into a
mighty outpouring of God's Spirit, complete with such biblical
manifestations as peace, healing, shaking, falling under the power
of God, laughter, and diversities of tongues. And it has continued
long after its modest beginnings, although I have gone on to minister in other parts of the world as God has directed my steps.

None of us had any idea what God was about to do at the Toronto Airport Vineyard. We opened the first meeting with about one hundred sixty people in attendance. Many people fell out under the power of God, but what surprised us most was the laughter. As people got drunk on the new wine of the Holy Spirit, wave after wave of great belly-laughter filled the auditorium. Amid what seemed to be all that chaos, people were being converted to Christ, and others were rededicating their lives. And that was just the first night.

Amid all that cacophony, people were going down under the power of God and coming up with incredible testimonies of what God had been doing while they were "resting" in the Spirit. There were testimonies of healing and deliverance. There were testimonies of those who had been powerfully launched into ministries and of others who had clearly heard God's call to go into the nations as End-Time evangelists. I had seen nothing like it before. It was what I had waited my whole life to experience. And here I was, a part of it!

I had been a student of church history, always attracted to the writings of the revivalists. I could suddenly imagine the awe experienced by some of those revivalists who had gone before, breaking spiritual ground and paving the way throughout history for what God had begun to pour out in Toronto.

The words written by John Wesley in his journal following an outpouring of the Holy Spirit on New Year's Eve, 1739, had taken on new life:

> At three in the morning, as we were confining in prayer, the power of God came upon us so mightily that many cried out in holy joy, while others were knocked to the ground.
>
> As soon as we recovered a little from awe and amazement at the presence of God, we broke out in one voice, "We praise Thee, O Lord God; we acknowledge Thee to be the Lord!"[1]

I recalled too the essence of the contents of a letter to George

Whitefield after the outbreak of the Welsh revival under Daniel Rowland:

> While one is praying, another is laughing; some howl and beat their hands together; others are weeping and groaning; and others are groveling on the ground in a swoon, making all kinds of antic postures; then they all laugh at once, and continue laughing for about a quarter of an hour. The power that continues with Rowland is uncommon.[2]

C. T. Studd's account of the Spirit's outpouring in Africa in 1914 sounded as current as the evening news. Studd had written:

> The whole place was charged with an electric current, men were falling, jumping, laughing, crying, singing, confessing, and some shaken terribly. It was a terrible sight . . .
>
> This particular one can best be described as a spiritual tornado. People were literally flung to the floor or over the forms, yet no one was hurt . . . as I led in prayer, the Spirit came down mightily sweeping the congregation. My whole body literally trembled with power. We saw a marvelous sight, people literally filled and drunk with the Spirit.[3]

Finally, it was A. W. Tozer's words that were quickened to me as I watched the sea of faces before me, reflecting the joy and the power and the presence of God:

> To have found God and still to pursue Him is the soul's paradox of love, scorned indeed by the too-easily-satisfied religionist, but justified in happy experience by the children of the burning heart. St. Bernard stated this holy paradox in a musical quatrain that will be instantly understood by every worshipping soul: "We taste Thee, O Thou Living Bread, and long to feast upon Thee still: We drink of Thee, the Fountainhead, and thirst our souls from Thee to fill."[4]

SPIRITUAL GROUNDBREAKING IN TORONTO

Now the experiences of the early revivalists in church history were coming alive in Toronto as God began to break up the fallow ground of spiritual apathy. And He did so in ways I had only read about. Yes, there was laughter—which I had seen previously at the meetings conducted by Rodney Howard-Browne. Yes, there were people slain in the Spirit—but again and again this manifestation of the power of God had been demonstrated among charismatic believers everywhere. Yes, there were people who were visibly shaking as the anointing lay heavily upon them. But this had been seen before—during the Quaker movement in England, for example.

What happened next in Toronto was something no one had seen before.

There were manifestations of animal sounds such as the roaring of lions. While such manifestations did not seem to mark the Toronto meetings when I personally ministered—and while they still do not—nevertheless the press and others in the Christian community became aware of this element of the renewal meetings in Toronto and had a field day. The religious media came to a meeting at another church and blew everything out of proportion, taking tiny sound bytes and making a big deal out of what I had only observed taking place on rare occasions. I actually believed the manifestation of animal noises represented a very small ripple on a very large pond—when in fact they would become the object of great controversy.

The meetings went on, night after night, with greater and greater manifestations of the power of God. The laughter intensified, as did the number of people who were slain in the Spirit under the power of God. Word must have gotten around fast, because by Sunday morning of the first week in Toronto, the sanctuary was packed.

The meetings were unusual also in that each one lasted longer than any of the other meetings I had ever conducted elsewhere. We usually got started around 7:30 P.M., and for the first four weeks the earliest those meetings ended was twenty minutes after

midnight! One night at 2:00 A.M. the Holy Spirit was not finished with us yet. Two hundred people were still in the
auditorium! At 3:00 A.M. some really powerful things began to
happen—and on many occasions the power of God seemed to
intensify among us at 3:00 A.M.

Sometimes there was so much laughter as we ministered that
what we were doing seemed to resemble more of a party than
church.

As one person observed, "Some of the ones who were
laughing the hardest and had the most fun said the laughter was
like the anesthesia for the surgery that the Holy Spirit was about
to perform on them, dredging up things that they had pressed
down because they were too painful to deal with. Now they were
coming up, and they were really beginning to get their healing.
It's like someone's throwing one big party!"

I can see how some of the meetings may have given the
impression of a party atmosphere. But why all that laughter?
Aside from my belief that God is changing the definition of
"church," I also believe that God wants us to have some fun.
Most people don't like church because they complain that it is
boring. God doesn't want church to be boring. He wants to
restore the excitement to church, much the same as when the
Holy Spirit first came among us in the first century. And He
wants to bring the prodigals back home.

I am convinced that Jesus wants us to celebrate when we come
to church—and enjoy the fact that the prodigals are suddenly
returning home in droves. We—the elder brothers and sisters of
those prodigals who have been away awhile—have been put in
charge of the welcoming committee.

So now the Lord wants us to throw a party for the prodigals
and celebrate their return to their Father's house. After all, this is
just the first phase of this great End-Time outpouring of the
Holy Spirit.

To date, we're just ankle-deep in it and splashing around. God
has more to pour out on us, but first He wants to throw a party
as He begins to clean us up. It's okay to party first; when it's
time, God will move on to more serious business. . . .

THE TASMANIAN DEVIL

The first Sunday morning service, Anni Shelton, the wife of my worship leader, Gary Shelton, told me the Lord had given her five names of people and words of knowledge concerning them. I gave her permission to give the words between worship and the message.

While Anni was still giving the words of knowledge, a man in the back row stood and began to shout: "Did you get my name? Did you get my name? I'm Taz—the Tasmanian Devil!"

This rather large, stocky man, with long hair and various tattoos, was apparently under the influence of alcohol. He continued to shout, interrupting Anni's ministry.

"I'll show you power!" he shouted.

As I heard those words, a burst of the anointing of God surged through me, and I stated, "No! I'll show *you* power—*the power of God!*"

Then, to the crowd of believers, I said, "Pay no attention to him; focus in on Jesus. The devil has overplayed his hand this morning, and now we are going to see the power of God!"

I asked for everyone present who had been feeling a strong anointing of the power of God on them to come forward for prayer. The front of the church quickly filled with people. I asked the Holy Spirit to fall upon us. Immediately people began to fall, shake, weep, laugh, or simply rest in deep peace.

Some of the men, in the meantime, had taken "Taz" out of the service. In one of the offices, they discovered that he had been stabbed multiple times just days earlier and that the knife wounds were still an angry pink. He had been hospitalized as a result of the stabbing and had almost died.

There in the office, as these men ministered to him, "Taz" gave his life to Jesus.

MIRACLES, SIGNS, AND WONDERS

God was pouring out His Spirit, and there were many signs and wonders. The Lord was moving among us so powerfully that John Arnott told me I couldn't go home until the Lord had finished what

He was doing in Toronto. This outpouring was what both John and I for many years had dreamed of and prayed for. And now here it was, happening to us. I had already called DeAnne twice and had each time extended the meetings for two or three more days. Now I was calling her for a third time, and she was, quite frankly, clueless as to what to make of all this Toronto outpouring business. She wanted me to come home.

John Arnott insisted that I stay. He even offered to fly DeAnne and the children up too, but we agreed this was a bad idea because of the childrens' school schedules. This was difficult, because in all our nineteen years of marriage DeAnne and I had only been apart for five days. Suddenly she was at home alone, caring for our twelve-year-old son, Joshua; Johannah, seven; Josiah, three; and one-year-old Jeremiah.

In a few more days I phoned her again and told her God was still not finished with me in Toronto. This time she broke down and cried.

"Don't cry, honey," I said, trying to soothe her ragged emotions. "We'll work something out."

Long after we ended our conversation, DeAnne continued to cry as she poured out her heart to God in prayer. "What does all this mean? Why is Randy having to stay for so long in Toronto? What does it mean for him? And what does all this mean to me and to our family? Lord, You have repeatedly provided for us miraculously; we have this beautiful new home, and now Randy isn't even here to enjoy it with me. And I don't want to raise our children as a single mother!"

Naturally emotionally troubled by these sudden, unexpected turn of events and by my absence, DeAnne cried out her petitions to God for the better part of an hour. Finally, when the heart-wrenching sobs subsided, the Lord impressed upon her to open her Bible. She had learned to find comfort from the Scriptures. She opened her Bible at random to read, and a passage of text from the Book of Isaiah leaped off the page:

> Listen to me, you islands; hear this you distant nations:
> Before I was born the LORD called me; from my birth he

has made mention of my name. He made my mouth like a sharpened sword, in the shadow of his hand he hid me; he made me into a polished arrow and concealed me in his quiver. He said to me, "You are my servant, Israel, in whom I will display my splendor." But I said, "I have labored to no purpose; I have spent my strength in vain and for nothing. Yet what is due me is in the LORD's hand, and my reward is with my God."

And now the LORD says—he who formed me in the womb to be his servant to bring Jacob back to him and gather Israel to himself, for I am honored in the eyes of the LORD and my God has been my strength—he says: "It is too small a thing for you to be my servant to restore the tribes of Jacob and bring back those of Israel I have kept. I will also make you a light for the Gentiles, that you may bring my salvation to the ends of the earth."

This is what the LORD says—the Redeemer and Holy One of Israel—to him who was despised and abhorred by the nation, to the servant of rulers: "Kings will see you and rise up, princes will see and bow down, because of the LORD, who is faithful, the Holy One of Israel, who has chosen you."

This is what the LORD says: "In the time of my favor I will answer you, and in the day of salvation I will help you; I will keep you and will make you to be a covenant for the people, to restore the land and to reassign its desolate inheritances, to say to the captives, 'Come out,' and to those in darkness, 'Be free!' They will feed beside the roads and find pasture on every barren hill. They will neither hunger nor thirst, nor will the desert heat or the sun beat upon them. He who has compassion on them will guide them and lead them beside springs of water."

—ISAIAH 49:1–10

DeAnne relates that at first she did not understand this text, but she felt an overwhelming sense of the presence of God as she read. She knew God's answer was contained in those ten verses. She received comfort in the fact that she now knew for certain that it was God keeping me in Toronto, and not me or John Arnott.

In the weeks that followed, it helped to know that DeAnne had received comfort from this passage of Scripture. While I was able to come home intermittently, the Toronto revival—which had become known as the "Toronto Blessing"—was still going strong and was demanding much of my time and attention. I did not know what to make of those verses for myself, since my faith level had still not risen to the point where I could see myself going to the nations. Toronto was one thing . . . *but the world?*

A Heart for Missions

Early on in what had been happening in Toronto, it became apparent to me that one of the themes of the Toronto Blessing was missions. While John Arnott and I were still busy trying to figure out what it was that God had been doing, it became apparent to both of us that whatever it was that God was doing, He planned to take it to the nations. He may have lit a fire in Toronto, but I quickly realized that the Lord intended to set the world ablaze, using Toronto as a torch to ignite other flames.

I also saw that what had been mostly a crowd of white Anglo-Saxon Protestants was diversifying and becoming a mixture of people from every tribe, race, and tongue. The pews were now filled with Iranians and Greeks, African-Americans and Chinese, Hispanics, Native Americans and Jews—and virtually everything in between. This was very exciting to me, as I believe it was exciting to God. John Arnott pointed out to me one day that, according to the United Nations, Toronto is one of the most ethnically diverse cities in the world. Looking out over the crowds who now attended our meetings, I could believe that statement was true. Once again, the meetings in Toronto seemed to resemble my idea of what the Azusa Street meetings must have been like, as for the first time the color line was washed away by the bloodline of Christ.

The crowds continued to grow, so that we had to move the meetings to Capitol Convention Hall to accommodate all the people. About seven months into the renewal, I began to preach a message called "Spend and Be Spent." It was actually a call to the mission field. I had been convicted to preach such a message after the Lord reminded me that major missionary expansions usually followed such periods of powerful outpouring as we were currently experiencing in Toronto. Suddenly I saw the connection between people responding to the call to missions and their being renewed by the Holy Spirit, who first had called them to love Jesus enough to respond to His calling them into the nations.

One of those who responded to the Lord's call to go to the nations was *me*.

NEW DOORS OPEN

In August 1994 I received an interesting prophetic word from Marc DuPont. It was surprising and very helpful to me. As a matter of fact, it had a profound influence upon me regarding my openness to working with those outside the Vineyard movement.

Marc DuPont's word was given to me one night as John and Carol Arnott, Wes and Stacy Campbell, Marc, and DeAnne and I were gathered together to minister to one another. Marc prophesied that in the near future I would be ministering more outside the Vineyard than inside the Vineyard churches. Until that time, and for twelve years since joining the Vineyard, I had ministered only in Vineyard churches. Now the Lord was saying, through Marc DuPont, that He was preparing to open doors for me to the Pentecostals, the Assemblies of God, and the Faith camp churches. Marc also told me that while there would still be open doors for me to minister in evangelical churches and the historical denominations, most of my future invitations to speak would come from the Pentecostal, Assemblies of God, and Faith camp churches.

Marc then said to me: "I know, I know; I've heard your testimony, and I know this word may sound bizarre to you. Just put it on the back burner for awhile and see what happens!"[5]

I didn't have to wait too long. Within two weeks I had

received an invitation to a Faith church, and in a few more weeks I was ministering in one of the largest Faith churches in New Jersey. I don't believe the ministry would have happened if I had not received that prophetic word from Marc.

THE CATCH THE FIRE CONFERENCE

In October 1994 John Arnott hosted the Catch the Fire Conference in Toronto, where I met David Carr of Elim Pentecostal Church in Surrey, England. He told me that the Lord had sent him to Toronto to speak to someone after he arrived. "Each time someone rose to speak, I would ask the Holy Spirit, 'Is this the man?' When you got up to speak, the Holy Spirit said, 'This is the man!'" David explained, as we discussed the unusual circumstances of our meeting. He told me that he had access to many parts of the world; if I would travel to minister, he could set up some meetings for me with the Pentecostals, the Assemblies, and the Faith camp. There was Marc DuPont's word to me again!

David Carr also invited me to come to England, which I later agreed to do.

At the Toronto conference I met Frank Sizer, a psychologist in private practice and a former Roman Catholic priest who had been instrumental in the healing movement of the 1970s Renewal. As he and I talked, I began to realize there was a need for some personal ministry. He experienced a deliverance. Following my ministry to him I felt God impressing me to tell Dr. Sizer that he was going to be restored to the healing ministry. Just eighteen months later Dr. Sizer came to St. Louis as a speaker at a healing conference at the Vineyard. He is now continuing his private practice in a limited manner but is also traveling and ministering in the area of healing ministry.

Following the Catch the Fire Conference, John Arnott, Wes Campbell, and I were invited to Yorba Linda, California, to meet with Todd Hunter, the acting national director of the Association of Vineyard Churches, all the regional overseers, and John Wimber in order to deal with some of the concerns that had already developed among the Vineyard churches regarding the strange manifestations that had marked the Toronto meetings. There were, in fact, as many as twenty subjects on the list to discuss at the meetings, but much time and attention were devoted to the issue of the animal noises. It was obvious to me that this had become a major concern for some of the Vineyard's regional overseers, although it did not seem as big a concern to Wes Campbell, John Arnott, and me. Apparently I had underestimated the seriousness of the issue, for it would later prove to be the singular cataclysmic event responsible for the disfellowshiping of the Toronto Vineyard.

THE TORONTO YEAR

The year I spent in Toronto had proven to be an exciting year of learning for me. From the outbreak of the renewal, God had riveted the cause of missions into my heart so powerfully that it was now unmistakable that I had been called to go into the nations as part of the End-Time gospel harvest.

This one theme ran through my ear: Missionary expansion always follows a period of revival in the church. I knew such power had been poured out in Toronto for just one reason—to equip the church to *go!*

I was now enjoying the satisfaction of seeing hundreds of young people respond to the invitation to go—to commit their lives to the mission field as evangelists, pastors, church planters, worship leaders, and missionaries. To see these young people step forward, weeping, in answer to the call had indeed made Toronto a blessing to me.

Another major theme of Toronto was that of refreshing, as thousands of the Father's weary servants flocked there, received His touch, and were sent away restored, refreshed, and ready to receive all God had for them. I thank God that He sent me to Toronto; going was pivotal to my future in ministry.

The following year proved to me that the Toronto Blessing was just the beginning and that the blessing would by no means be confined to Toronto. . . .

An Unforgettable Year

In 1995 I saw more healings occur than I saw during the sum of all my years in ministry. God sent me many places that year. I held meetings in Melbourne, Florida; in Charlotte, North Carolina; in Pasadena, California; in Guatemala City, Guatemala; in Louisville, Kentucky; in Hendersonville, Tennessee; in Philadelphia, Pennsylvania. And everywhere there were reports of healings, deliverance, salvation, and the powerful presence of God. I was blown away again and again by what God was doing in our midst.

Everything about 1995 was not completely wonderful. One of the most difficult things for me during this year was the disfellowshiping of the Toronto Airport Vineyard from the Association of Vineyard Churches.

I first became aware of the possibility that this might happen while I was preaching at Deliverance Evangelistic Church in Philadelphia. Twice, over a period of two days, I was called out of the meetings for an emergency phone call just minutes before the services were scheduled to begin. I was notified that the disfellowshiping of Toronto was under discussion during the first of these telephone calls.

I couldn't believe it was true! I was also notified that Todd Hunter, the national overseer for the Association of Vineyard Churches, was on his way to see me.

I began to realize that the Toronto Blessing might wind up costing me my relationship with the Vineyard—a relationship that was very important to me emotionally. I had been part of the Vineyard since September 1984 when there were only fifty Vineyard churches. The one I had started in Illinois had been one of the first Vineyards to be established east of Denver, Colorado. I felt as if God was asking me to sacrifice my relationship with the Vineyard—my Isaac—on the altar of renewal. As I cried out to God in prayer, I told Him that I was so convinced that this revival was of Him, I was willing to stand for it—even if it meant being disfellowshiped. "I'm willing to pay the price!" I told the Lord. I also told Him that if I was asked by the Vineyard to break my relationship with John Arnott or to stop my involvement with the renewal, I would have to leave the denomination because I knew for certain that God had called me to Toronto.

After I had received the peace of God through prayer and my course had been set as a result of hearing from the Holy Spirit, I contacted John Arnott to find out what had been going on. He told me that John Wimber, Bob Fulton, Gary Best, and Todd Hunter had already met with Wes Campbell and his staff and that the meeting with these top Vineyard officials had been very distressing to Wes. Wes was left wondering whether he would be able to stay in the denomination and elected to take a "wait-and-see" attitude.

The next night I again spoke to John Arnott. The Toronto Airport Vineyard had just been disfellowshiped from the Association of Vineyard Churches. I couldn't believe what I was hearing!

I was upset and hurt by this action. I was also in such pain from a physical condition related to the stress of this event that I was forced to stay in bed for the next three days. I rose only at night to preach, then returned to bed immediately afterward. Friends contacted me from both the Vineyard and from Toronto, and I felt caught in the middle . . . much as if I were a child caught in the crossfire of a divorce.

I was grieved by the entire matter—grieved by the decision of the Vineyard's leadership, grieved at the reasons given for the decision, grieved at the way the entire matter had been handled, grieved over the ramifications of the decision on the renewal as it continued in Toronto and elsewhere, and grieved over the ramifications of the decision upon the Association of Vineyard Churches.

I felt uncertain about my own future. I also didn't know whether or not to remain in a Vineyard Church. I resolved that I, too, would wait and see how the Vineyard's decision to disfellowship Toronto would impact me.

Todd Hunter never did come to see me. We later met out in California when I spoke at the Let the River Flow conference with him, Gary Best, and John Wimber in Anaheim. Ironically, I flew to Anaheim after completing my involvement in John

Arnott's church to commemorate the second anniversary of the Toronto Blessing.

I have agonized somewhat over the fact that the waters of outpouring which had at first seemed a glorious and unmistakable blessing were now churned with the whitecaps of controversy and discontent. Not everyone, it seems, was as pleased as I had been at what God had been doing. While it is not my wish to disparage or call into question anyone else's motives, it was now painfully apparent to me that this new move of God would not be embraced by everyone.

But I have experienced the pinnacle of excitement over what God has been doing there and my involvement in it. I have been blessed by the unity expressed in the hearts of believers who have come together in Toronto for the sole purpose of worshiping God and being touched by Him. I have been touched by the love of God as again and again He has knelt down from heaven and swept through lives at the altar in Toronto. Whether people were healed, knocked down, endued with power, or simply blessed, the fact remains that after these souls were touched by God in Toronto, they were never the same afterward.

After all, revivals throughout history had come under the scrutiny and scorn of those who could not understand what God appeared to be doing in their midst. I could recall the words of Jonathan Edwards after just such an attack against his ministry:

> Those who stand wondering at this strange work, not knowing what to make of it, and refusing to receive it—and ready . . . to speak contemptibly of it . . . would do well to tremble at Paul's word (Acts 13:41): "Behold, you scoffers, and marvel, and perish. For I am accomplishing a work in your days, a work which you will never believe though someone should describe it to you." Let all to whom this work is a cloud and darkness . . . take heed that it not be their destruction while it gives light to God's Israel.

Revival doesn't come cheap. There is a cost to count in pursuing more of God. Some of you reading this book have already counted the cost and have gladly been paying it; some of you may right now be in the midst of such a season of counting the cost. Are you willing to let God take you out of your comfort zone and lead you forth into an End-Time anointing? Please consider what I am about to say before you volunteer, because this is an extremely dangerous thing to set your hand to. God wants to empower you, and He is fully capable of doing it. But it may cost you an awful lot of comfort and security. Do you want the anointing even if it costs you everything? Do you want the presence of God so much that you will press on to receive it?

You will not have more power until you are dissatisfied with where you are spiritually. You will not receive more power until you *want* more. You will not have greater intimacy with Jesus until you become dissatisfied with your current relationship with Him. Jesus is using a nobody like me, "little ol' me," for His glory because I press Him for more. I want to tell you, *"There's more!* God has more to pour out on you! You can have more of the anointing . . . more of Him! But in order to receive it, you must let Him have more of you!"

By pressing in for many years, I have received more of God, and I'm so thankful for that, that I can hardly express it in words. But it has cost me some things along the way.

During the long and difficult years of preparation in the wilderness, God taught me that the anointing *always* costs something. There is something about following Jesus that involves sacrifice. It always exacts a high price. In the wilderness years I discovered that the cost of true discipleship involves more than economics; sometimes it costs relationships, even allegiances. I learned that sometimes there will be costs as well to family roles, since rarely do one's family members fully understand the call of God. And I learned that not all of those who pray for revival to come to their cities and to their churches will like it or feel like blessing it once it comes—especially if it comes in an entirely new manner from the last outpouring on earth.

As in the case of Toronto. . . .

SEVEN

MOSCOW

See, I have placed before you an open door that no one can shut.

—REVELATION 3:8

W HEN I WAS IN COLLEGE I met a man whose own call to the mission field impacted me in a powerful way. His name was Nobuo Tanaka.[1] I have never forgotten him or the way God used him to influence and inspire me with the same zeal for global evangelism that marked his own life. Now that God had begun to launch me forth into the global ministry arena, I often thought of Nobuo and of the tremendously high price he paid to follow God's call to *go!*

You see, Nobuo Tanaka gave up everything dear to him—all that he had—to follow the call of God upon his life. Nobuo, the son of a dirt-poor minister in post-World War II Japan, had worked hard during his school years to earn grades good enough to win a scholarship so he could study medicine. His burning desire was to pull himself up out of a lifestyle of poverty and scorn in which he had been raised. And he did it. He won an all-expense-paid scholarship to a leading university to study to become a surgeon. But then Jesus knocked upon the door of Nobuo's heart, and he was so overwhelmed by the knowledge of how the Lord had planned to use his life that Nobuo gave his heart to Jesus. When the offering plate came around to him during this same service, Nobuo put the most valuable thing he owned into the plate—his future. And he never looked back.

INSPIRED TO MISSIONS

When Nobuo and I met, he was already studying for the ministry at a Baptist college and preparing to enter Asbury Theological Seminary. I could see that he was truly brilliant. He and I were roommates as well as friends. One night as we sat up late, studying, I noticed that Nobuo had long scars on his abdomen, chest, and one of his legs. When I inquired about the scars, Nobuo told me his story. I never forgot it.

Nobuo's mother had died of starvation during the post-war American occupation of Japan after World War II. His father was one of the few Christian ministers in Japan. To be a Christian pastor in the Japan of the 1940s and 1950s brought scorn, rejection, and separation from family, friends, and countrymen. If found to be a Christian, your Japanese brothers and sisters would refuse to serve you in shops and restaurants. They would scorn and ridicule you to the point of refusing to let you drink from public drinking fountains.

"I literally saw people spit in our food in restaurants once they learned my parents were Christians," Nobuo confided to me that night more than twenty-five years ago as I listened in fascination.

"So I decided as a young boy that I was never going to be a Christian! I decided, 'I am going to get out of poverty, and I am going to make something of my life!' And what was the way out? Education!"

Nobuo Tanaka graduated as valedictorian of one of the largest high schools in Japan. By that time he had studied both karate and judo. He received a scholarship to attend college and another that would not only pay his way through graduate school and residency to become a surgeon but would also give him spending money. All he had to do to receive the package deal was sign on the dotted line. And up to the point of graduating from high school he had still not accepted Jesus Christ as his Savior.

At nineteen years of age, between high school and college, Nobuo attended his dad's little church, and the Holy Spirit unzipped heaven and began to convict him. Nobuo already knew that if he became a Christian, it would mean that he would also have to give up his plan to become a surgeon and become a minister instead.

One of the greatest offerings ever taken in the annals of Christian history was taken that day. Scholarship in pocket—the Holy Spirit convicted Nobuo: "Will you give Me your life?" As the offering plate was passed down the row, a battle raged within Nobuo. Finally, the offering plate before him, Nobuo reached inside his coat pocket and pulled out the scholarship. He laid it gently on the top of the pile of paper money and coins, and as it was taken away, so went his dreams to become a successful surgeon.

He accepted Jesus that night and answered *yes* to God's one question: "Will you give Me your life?" Nobuo Tanaka was willing to sacrifice everything he valued on earth for something he valued more—the call of God.

Without realizing it, Nobuo Tanaka had given me a key to success that night so long ago. It's simple—that one question, the question that will change your powerless life into a powerful one, filled with purpose. The Holy Spirit is asking those called to ministry the same question today as then: "Will you give Me your life?"

THOSE SCARS

When Nobuo said yes, he really meant it. Following the Holy Spirit's leading just after his call to the ministry, Nobuo Tanaka took what little bit of money he had and booked passage by ship to a small island, Aogashima, off the coast of Japan. The people of that island had never heard the gospel. Aogashima had no natural port, so Nobuo asked a fisherman to take him to the island on his fishing boat. Because there was no place to come ashore with his boat, the fisherman signaled to shore for a smaller boat to pick up Nobuo and take him the rest of the way to the island.

Once he got there, he located the most visible spot on the island, opened his Bible, and began to preach Jesus. The powers of darkness amassed against him, and a group of angry young men attacked and overwhelmed him. But even though Nobuo was a martial arts expert, there were more assailants than he could handle by himself. He was stabbed by one of his assailants and left for dead. Many of the villagers did not want Nobuo on the island, and as he lay on the ground, they began to harass him, hitting and kicking him.

A good Samaritan picked him up, took him home, and nursed him back to health. He then embarked on a fast, crying out to Jesus to give him the souls of the islanders for the kingdom of God. At the end of the fast, he returned to where he had been overwhelmed. Once more, he preached. There he stood, alone, nineteen years old, Bible open, preaching the gospel. This time the Holy Spirit fell, and a gradual revival of Christian faith took place in Aogashima. Many people—including the young men who had previously tried to kill Nobuo—received Jesus and were converted.

When it came time for Nobuo to return to the Japanese mainland, an older woman came to him with an offering as precious as the one he had recently given. She gave him the money she had saved for many years—money she had planned to use to realize her goal of traveling to Tokyo to see that grand city for herself before she died. Instead, she brought the money wrapped inside a napkin to Nobuo and said: "I want you to take this and use it to do God's work."

"I can't take this!" Nobuo objected.

"You must take it!" the woman insisted. With tears streaming down her face, she said, "I no longer want to see Tokyo now that I am about to see the New Jerusalem!"

So Nobuo took the money and served the Lord in the Sunday school of a church with the sacrificial offering of that little Japanese woman.

That's what I learned from Nobuo—the power of sacrifice and how God honors it. Nobuo graduated from seminary and married a Japanese-American woman. He was an associate pastor in a large Methodist church, and his wife had a good job as a physical therapist when Nobuo got word that his father's health was failing. His father had requested that he return to Japan to take over his church. Again, sacrifice. He walked away from that associate pastorate, from that large salary, from the lifestyle of comfort he and his wife had worked so hard to establish. He returned to Japan, and for a number of years I lost track of him.

One day not too long ago a Japanese man came to my church in St. Louis. "Have you ever heard of Nobuo Tanaka?" I asked, hoping to find my friend.

"Yes," the man replied. "He is one of the most respected pastors in Japan today."

SPEND AND BE SPENT

Sacrifice. Spend and be spent. Words we Christians don't like to hear. But, like Nobuo, the early church knew the power of sacrifice as well as the immeasurable rewards. Again and again God has poured out His Spirit, using men like Nobuo Tanaka to shake the earth.

God has always raised up people to bring renewal and revival, but first it has often cost them something dear. At times it has cost them their lives. Let me give you some examples from church history.

A wealthy young man had a visitation from Jesus, and suddenly this twenty-year-old son of a Catholic merchant saw the true condition of the church—run down, powerless, full of hypocrisy, lacking both zeal and a heart for the Lord. This dismayed the young Francis, who walked away from the family fortune to follow the call of God upon his life. Before long, he was so on fire for the Lord that he had a small following. He and other young men like him cast off their fine apparel in favor of simple brown woolen robes, tied at the waist with ropes instead of belts. Soon there were hundreds of followers who went throughout Europe, preaching the gospel. No one tried to beat them or steal from them because they owned nothing. When the Black Plague swept through Europe, the inhabitants of entire cities died. It was those young men in plain brown robes who nursed the sick, burned the dead bodies, and took no thought for their own lives. The movement finally received a name—the Franciscans. The young man who founded the movement was the man we know of now as St. Francis of Assisi. He brought revival to the Catholic church and established a place in church history.[2]

A thousand young men followed Ignatius Loyola, a great man who was known for his intense prayer life. The Loyola movement attracted those, like its founder, who were committed to a lifestyle of prayer and seeking God. Loyola himself was martyred, giving his life for the cause of Christ as he ministered to the unbelievers of China.[3]

Martin Luther, the father of Protestantism, may have viewed his role in church events more as one of recovering lost doctrines than of starting anything new. His recovery of the doctrine of justification by grace through faith alone shook the church to its very foundations, and what emerged was the battle cry, *Sola Scriptura, Sola Fida, Sola Christe*—"Scripture alone, faith alone, Christ alone." The focus became doctrinal purity instead of missions, and much arguing resulted over hair-splitting during the first two hundred years of Protestantism—only a hundred missionaries were sent out into the world in that period.[4] The world had entered an era known as Protestant scholasticism, with theologians suddenly arguing about such esoteric issues as how many angels can sit on the head of a pin, instead of going forth with the gospel into all the world. There was a need for restored zeal if these Protestants were to continue.

Count Nikolaus Ludwig von Zinzendorf was a Pietist. Influenced by the Puritans of England, the Pietists were young professors in the universities of Moravia and were teaching something new and different—it was not enough to have right doctrine; not enough to have a right confession of faith. What was missing was a heartfelt religion and a relationship in which one could actually "feel" the presence of God. The Pietists advocated small home groups where there was high accountability, as well as much Bible study and a strong devotional life. Count von Zinzendorf had been greatly influenced by August Franc and Phillippe Spainer.[5]

Von Zinzendorf had heard of Hussites who were being persecuted throughout Moravia for their faith. He opened his palace, called *Herrnhut,* as a place of refuge for the persecuted. The name of the palace means "the Lord's watch." Inside the safety of its walls, people flocked from different theological persuasions.

Von Zinzendorf's vision was the dream of unity among streams of Christian belief. But the great experiment would not succeed. Back-biting, bickering, and gossiping soon broke out among the inhabitants of Herrnhut; to remedy the infighting the count suggested prayer. One night as communion was being celebrated, the Holy Spirit fell, and there was a powerful impartation of the Spirit. The prayer meeting lasted twenty-four hours a day, all week long, for one hundred years. The members of this little group never tried to push themselves; yet in the first twenty-five years of that revival at Herrnhut, more missionaries were sent forth from that small band of believers than all of Protestantism in the previous two hundred years!

What was the difference? The message of a personal experience with God—not just knowing about Him. Out of Count von Zinzendorf's vision for a united body of Christ came the Moravian church, and their sole object was to win for the Lamb that was slain the rewards for His suffering—souls everywhere.

A young man, a priest of the Anglican church, traveled to Georgia in America to preach to Indians there. During the shipboard journey, a terrible storm hit, and even the most seasoned sailors aboard despaired of life. The young priest noticed a group of about sixty Moravians who were caught up in worship of the Lord. Joy and peace were written on these faces, yet the young man from England was moved with fear by the danger all around him. "Aren't you afraid?" he asked one of the Moravians.

"No, we are ready to meet God," the Moravian answered, adding, "Are you afraid?"

"Yes, I am," the young man answered truthfully.

"Don't you know that Jesus died for your sins?" responded the Moravian.

"I know Jesus died for the sins of the world," the Englishman answered.

"Yes, but do you know that Jesus died for your sins?"

The Anglican priest failed in his missionary trip to America. On shipboard to return to England, he wrote in his journal: "I went to America to save the Indians and realized that I needed someone to save me."

The young man's name was John Wesley, who, after a dramatic encounter with the Holy Spirit, would establish the Methodist denomination and turn the world upside down for Christ.[6]

WHITE UNTO HARVEST

I thought about these men—Nobuo and those who had gone before him . . . Francis of Assisi, John Wesley, as well as others I had learned about who had shaped and changed the landscape of the church as we know it. Now I was about to embark on one of the greatest seasons of ministry I had ever known, and I couldn't help but think about those from history—what it had cost them, what they had accomplished for Christ, and what I was doing even attempting to take Christ to the nations. I could understand how God would use a Nobuo or a Francis or a Wesley or a Count von Zinzendorf. But me—little ol' me?

Why not me? Did I not have this burning desire within me for world evangelism? And if I had it, where had it come from if not from God? I could see that the fields were white and ready for harvest—and I believed that it would take every one of us with a call for world evangelism to go and get the job done. *So why not me?*

Whether or not I could comprehend all of what God was doing, it appeared that He was honoring my zeal for world evangelism. Because again and again in the meetings in Toronto and elsewhere, He had unzipped heaven and poured out the power of the Holy Spirit. I believed we were smack dab in the middle of revival—right where I wanted to be.

God had begun to speak prophetically all around me regarding this great wave of revival that I was beginning to ride. Everywhere there were demonstrations of the move of God. In Toronto, a very respected member of John Arnott's church shared a word with us that John and I both bore witness to: "The Lord said, 'I am coming to you gently so that you will not be afraid when I come in power.'" I looked at John after hearing it, and remembering all the bodies of those laid out around me who had "fallen out" under the power of the Holy Spirit, I asked, "Is *this* gentle?"

I'm glad the Lord did it this way first, because a more powerful way would have freaked me out. Falling under the power was about all I could have handled at the time. Yet I do believe that this first wave of outpouring will be gentle as God ministers to believers; the second wave will be full of power, abundant with signs and wonders, because it will be a harvest to the lost.

And the fields *are* ready . . . white unto harvest. It's time.

NEW DOORS OPEN

So why was I doing what I was doing? Because I knew without question that I had been called to global evangelism. I had just done the second anniversary service to commemorate the outpouring in Toronto. That meeting in Toronto was one of the most powerful I had attended in some time. It was also one of the most demonstrative, including some rather bizarre examples of prophetic intercession and manifestations of drunkenness, laughing, weeping, and even some playful "punching" by some of the speakers—all outside the realm of my personal comfort zone. But God had never been known to check with me for what was within my comfort zone before He began to move, and I tried not to ask Him to limit His activity to my personal comfort level. Right after Toronto, I flew to Anaheim, California, to speak at the Vineyard's Let the River Flow conference.

Following the Anaheim conference, Wimber and I met with Todd Hunter and Bob Fulton. They shared their concerns, and I shared mine. After it was determined that I was not under any kind of disciplinary action for my part in the Toronto meetings, Wimber told me he was pleased with most of what he had heard about my renewal meetings. He said he appreciated the way I had made myself accountable to Todd Hunter. I felt good about the six-hour meeting when it was over; it had been very constructive. I had explained to those present that God had begun to open doors for me to minister in Pentecostal, Assemblies, and Faith camp churches. It was understood that I would have the freedom to participate in any of these meetings, and John Wimber blessed me to work with these new open doors.

THE MOSCOW BLESSING

In March 1996 I went to Moscow, Russia, to lead some of the most exciting meetings I had participated in to date. The Russian leaders were excited also, and claimed afterward that the meetings were "historic." They kept stating that what had happened at the meetings would "profoundly affect the Russian community." The meetings had the handprint of God upon them from the very beginning. This is the story of what has become known as "the Moscow Blessing."

In April 1990 I was powerfully touched by the Holy Spirit when I saw Mike Bickle receive a 1.2 million-dollar offering to purchase Bibles for Russia. In the midst of that offering I began to weep and received a strong impression: "You are going to go to Russia, and you are to take your worship team." When I returned to St. Louis following the meeting, I had been so moved by the experience that I told the worship team about it. The whole idea of our ministering seemed impossible—even ludicrous—since we had only about fifty people in our church at the time. So I put the experience on the back burner, where it would remain for nearly four years.

Then I met Howard Foltz while at Regent University in 1994.

I was there to preach the message, "Spend and Be Spent," during renewal meetings there that had a strong missions theme. Howard invited me to his office, where we talked about missions with a particular emphasis on Russia. He gave me a video to watch about Russia. When I returned home I popped the video into the VCR and watched it with DeAnne, who is not usually very excited about missions. We were both moved to tears. After viewing it, DeAnne said she too believed I should take a group from our church to Russia to minister. For several months I played the video for pastors I knew and encouraged them to contact Howard Foltz to find out more about missions opportunities in Russia.

One day in January 1995, while praying, I felt impressed by God to ask Him for a hundred thousand dollars to be used for whatever He wanted me to do with that amount. I had no idea what He had in mind—but I prayed as He directed. Within a matter of weeks, He made me aware that the money would be used for a ministry trip to Russia.

Later the same month I announced to our church that I would be going to Russia and that the worship team would be going with me. I explained that, in the meantime, the worship team would be learning to sing phonetically in Russian. I further explained that we would be seeking a ministry couple to leave behind. It was apparent that no one in our church felt called to the Russian mission field.

Three days later, in Melbourne, Florida, I met Keith. He and his Polish-born wife had been back in the United States for about a year after working in Russia. "What did you do in Russia?" I asked Keith, who had requested that I pray for him "for guidance."

"We were involved in a church planting," he said.

I was speechless.

When I could finally get myself together, I pressed for more details, and Keith told me: "I was the youth leader of the first church planted by Americans in Moscow."

"I'll pray for you," I said, "and after this meeting I want to have breakfast with you!"

That meeting proved to be a divine connection. At breakfast I shared my vision for taking a ministry team to Russia, as well as how God had called me to the nations.

"The Lord even gave my wife a Scripture to confirm my call to world evangelism—Isaiah 49:1–10," I told Keith and his wife, Iwona. When I said that, Iwona dropped her head down onto the table and kept it there for a moment. When she raised her head, she said, "I can't believe it! Isaiah 49:6 is my life verse!"

"What did you do in Russia?" I asked her then.

"I trained English-speaking worship teams how to sing phonetically in Russian."

Again, I was speechless . . . blown away by this doubly divine appointment.

From that meeting Keith and Iwona joined our ministry team, and from that point on the Moscow trip quickly began to gel.

IGOR, LAVERNE, AND ILENE

Then I met Igor Tsupek, and Laverne and Ilene Campbell through another series of divine appointments. What an experience this was turning out to be! Laverne and Ilene had great connections in Russia, and they introduced me to Igor, who had started a school in Russia that in the course of just eighteen months had sent out over seven hundred students who had, in turn, started about a thousand churches. I was deeply touched as Igor shared the need for new churches and the critical nature of taking advantage of the new spiritual openness in Russia.

The three were added to our team, and now we were ready for Moscow. Initially my plan was to host a conference for the young church planters that Igor had previously sent out from his school. Igor felt this would be of great encouragement to them. We also wanted to raise money to underwrite the cost of new church plantings by students who were trained to go out but needed support from sponsoring churches in America. I had hoped to see at least forty churches planted from our efforts. At the time we believed this could be done for a thousand dollars per student, which would pay for crusade advertisement, facility rentals, and a year's salary for each young Russian church planter. Our plan was to bring one thousand of these church planters to Moscow for a renewal meeting in October 1995. And our financial goal was to raise a hundred thousand dollars.

We didn't make that goal.

We also realized that our plan did not represent the full will of God—so we began to seek more guidance in order to make the right adjustments. As we prayed, God revealed one of the problems facing the church in Russia: Now that religious freedom was becoming a reality, there was division among the different church groups that were beginning to emerge. Jealousy, suspicion, competition, and lack of cooperation plagued many churches.

It was determined that if we only brought Igor Tsupek's men, what we were trying to do would be unwittingly identified with just Igor and his work in Russia. This would only create more division within the Moscow Christian community. Therefore, we decided to invite all key ministries, denominations, and mission organizations in Russia to participate in our meetings.

Our preliminary meeting was held in Moscow in October 1995 and proved to be strategic; we would have been totally unprepared for the Moscow renewal had we not first held this important meeting. Four more days of meetings followed with leaders of several streams of the Christian church in Moscow. Most of our efforts were spent trying to remove the fears that existed of what we were doing within the registered Pentecostal denomination. That group did not attend our conference, although we are hopeful that they will change their position and allow their pastors to attend future conferences we intend to hold in Moscow.

It was during these meetings in Moscow in the fall of 1995 that we discovered an important key to receiving what God would pour out: "One man's flesh is another man's spirit." What one did not receive, another would receive with joy. Although not everyone received what we were trying to do in Moscow, the meetings were nevertheless successful because of their foundation of unity in the body of Christ. Rather than circumventing the existing church authorities in Moscow, we included them; we invited the leadership, and they in turn agreed to invite their pastors to our meetings. The only group not represented in what we were trying to do in Moscow was the Russian Orthodox church—and that was simply because we had no contacts within that denomination to provide an open door for us to include their leadership in our conference.

The renewal conference was held in March 1996, with pastors, church planters, worship leaders, and the leaders of movements in attendance. We paid for everything as a service of love to the Moscow leadership. Ten days before the conference, we realized that due to inflation we were approximately thirty thousand dollars short—and if we didn't raise that amount, only five hundred of our Russian brothers and sisters would be able to attend the conference.

So I humbled myself. Fresh out of fund-raising ideas and out of time, I went to some of my ministry friends and asked for their help. Rodney Howard-Browne committed five thousand dollars, as did John Arnott from Toronto Airport Christian Fellowship. Right before our departure we received another offering from Rodney Howard-Browne that added fifty-five hundred dollars. Now only a few thousand dollars short of what it would take to host a thousand at the conference, we took what we had, and the Lord blessed it: Nine hundred and eighty Russian leaders were able to attend.

The renewal conference had actually exceeded our expectations. We had worried that, regardless of how phonetically correct our worship team could sing in Russian, the Muscovites would not be able to understand the words they sang. The comments we received afterward went mostly like this: "We thought they were Russians!"

When asked about the importance of the worship team's singing in Russian, one of the Russian leaders responded, "The apostle Paul said it is better to say five words in a language you understand than ten thousand in one you can't."

The anointing fell very heavily in each of the meetings we held in Moscow, and one pastor came back to us with this report: "I could do little more than weep as I told my congregation about the worship and the anointing in the Moscow meetings."

The meetings were now known as "the Moscow Blessing." And the fruit was nothing short of wonderful.

INTO THE NATIONS

Next we spent twenty-one days in Norway, ministering in Trondheim, Oslo, and Bergen. Each time we were blessed with the presence of God in our meetings. While we were in Bergen a man who had been disabled for almost twenty years was healed. Then it was on to England and Northern Ireland during the month of May. Many were healed during these meetings, and countless others testified that they were empowered with a fresh anointing of the Holy Spirit. In Belfast the mother of our hosts was healed of glaucoma that had destroyed the retinas of her eyes. Before we prayed together she had only peripheral vision; after praying for about thirty minutes, she was able to read the fine print of her Bible. Praise God!

Our final trip of 1996 was to Argentina, where my team and I spent nine days meeting with key leaders of the revival there—including Omar Cabrera, Carlos Annacondia, and Claudio Freidzon. During that first meeting the Lord worked it out so that I was invited to speak at a pastors' meeting as well as at the second annual pastors' clinic held by the Central Baptist Church in Buenos Aires. While at this church I met Pablo Bottari, the man responsible for training those who worked in the deliverance tent at Carlos Annacondia's meetings.

Before my arrival in Argentina, I had been prepared to spend only about an hour with these great men of God; instead, I was able to spend three hours with Freidzon, Annacondia, and Cabrera; an additional three hours with Pablo Deiros of the Central Baptist Church; and three more hours with Victor Lorenzo, a key person in Argentina who has dealt with the subject of spiritual mapping. A correspondent of one of the largest Christian newspapers in Argentina also interviewed me for two hours. Not only did God open doors for me in Argentina, but He also blew me away with the favor and grace poured out during the nine days there.

I had taped each of my interviews with these great spiritual leaders as I met with them in Argentina. When I arrived home and listened to the tapes once again, I began to realize how important it had been for me to record the interviews. I wanted to make the tapes available to the rest of the world so that others could understand in historical and personal context what God was doing in this great Argentinean outpouring.

The testimonies were so powerful that the person who transcribed them wound up committing her life to Christ after simply hearing them. The typist came under the conviction of the Holy Spirit by the power of the testimonies and was born again.

THE BITTER AND THE SWEET

While my heart has grieved over the disfellowshiping of what was formerly the Toronto Airport Vineyard, I can only thank God for extending His matchless grace to me to continue moving freely in and out of various "camps." The renewal that God sovereignly chose to birth in Toronto is so much bigger that no one church or denomination could contain it. Any attempt to box it would surely fail. This powerful move of God we're in the midst of today is born, not of works, but of relationship—relationship between the Father and His children. It is born not of legalism, but of grace.

Thus, it is my prayer that every person on earth may one day be able to experience what I have personally tasted of the grace of God. My heart is elated at how God has borne me up and over the events of the Toronto disfellowshiping, lifting me above any trace of bitterness. And He has given me the sweetness of seeing my call to world evangelism begin to be fulfilled.

My heart is full of the knowledge of the sovereignty of God— so full of awe at what He is doing that it continually blows me away just to think of it. What He began to pour out in Toronto has moved across the globe—and this is no small brush fire whipped about by a whimsical wind that changes direction by random. *This is a blazing inferno!*

INTO THE NATIONS

I THANK GOD FOR WHAT He is doing throughout the earth today. I thank Him for the fire that broke out in Toronto and spread around the globe. At times it seems to me that I have been conscripted by the Holy Spirit into His service to take that fire to the nations. And I realize that what began as the Toronto Blessing is only a part of a much greater worldwide revival that is being poured out in this present move of God. I am grateful to have lived long enough to have seen it and even more grateful for the opportunity to take part in it.

Many of you who are reading this book have a call upon your lives to help fulfill the Great Commission. The church of Jesus

Christ must be willing to *go!* To you, I say, "Go! But wait until He sends you! God has a plan and a purpose; but first He has a process. He will first take you through the training and equipping necessary to prepare you to fulfill the call He has placed upon you. He will make you ready, and then—at the appropriate time—He will launch you. Don't get ahead of God. Don't try to make it happen on your own. *Trust Him,* and He will open doors for you that no man can close!"

Remember that it is out of relationship that this powerful new move of God is born. As He continues to shape and perfect your relationship with Him, He will increase accordingly the anointing He has placed upon your life. When you are completely equipped to perform what He has called you to do on earth, He will release you to *go!*

I would like to provide these guidelines as encouragement to those of you who wish to be used by God:

- Cultivate an attitude of humility.
- Pursue unity within the body of Christ.
- Develop a secret prayer life with God.
- Become grounded in His Word.
- Pay attention to the promptings of your heart.
- Fast and pray.
- Visit those places and people where and in whom God is pouring out His Spirit in an unusual manner.
- Have the patience necessary to wait for the fulfillment of prophetic words with which your spirit bears witness.
- Accept the sovereignty of God.

APPENDIX I

FIVE-STEP
PRAYER MODEL

THE FOLLOWING five-step prayer model was developed by the Vineyard leadership for use when ministering healing. I have found it to be helpful; therefore, I am sharing it with you:

1. *Interview the person.* Try to find out what is wrong. Listen on two levels—in the Spirit, quietly praying in tongues if you have a prayer language, and if not, pray in English: "Oh, God, oh, God, oh, God! Help! Help!" Listen in the natural. God may give you a word of knowledge as to the root causes of the pain, that is, emotional, psychosomatic, organic physical problem,

121

spiritual problem related to sin, and so forth.

2. *Make a diagnostic decision.* Ask yourself, *Is the root of the problem emotional or spiritual? A sin problem? An afflicting spirit? Or purely physical?*

3. *Speak to the condition.* Pray directly for the effect. For instance, pray, "I command that back to straighten in the name of Jesus."

4. *Reinterview.* See what's happening. Pray based on what you're told; continue to pray if a healing appears to be in process. If nothing has started yet, determine if there is a need to pray differently. Or, if the person seems to have been healed, stop praying.

5. *Give a post-prayer directive.* In some cases, if the problem is related to sin, share the Scripture passage where Jesus said, "Stop sinning or something worse may happen to you" (John 5:14).

APPENDIX II

PROPHETIC WORDS AND OTHER CIRCUMSTANCES PERTAINING TO RENEWAL/ REVIVAL AND ME

I N APRIL 1994 I met with John Wimber to discuss what was happening in my life. During this meeting John asked me why I was doing what I was doing. He asked me if God had told me to do this, or was I doing it because I liked it? He was concerned about my family and advised me not to spend more than six days per month in renewal unless I could prove to him that this was what God was calling me to do. Our discussion proved most helpful.

For the next several months I reflected on this question, "Why are you doing this?" I was forced to reflect upon why I believed God had called me to minister in the renewal. While on vacation in July, for the first time I put together all the things that had caused me to believe God was calling me to work in renewal. All that follows, except the last prophecy from Marc Dupont, had occurred prior to the last week in July 1994.

1. Prophetic dream in 1984 or 1985

A young couple in my church had the same exact dream on the same night. At that time I was either in the Baptist church or pastoring a small group of people in Marion, Illinois, while new in the Vineyard. They dreamed I was standing on a stage in front of a large crowd of six to seven hundred people and said, "Come, Holy Spirit." Everyone, including the young couple, fell to the ground. They told me this dream right after they had it. I never forgot it, did not try to self-fulfill it, and did not always believe that one day it would come to pass. I am still waiting, but I am much more expectant now than at any time during the past.

2. Prophetic word given by Ginny Sprately on July 13, 1989

At the time I was moving in little power, and the Vineyard in St. Louis was very small. Ginny never gave this word to me until I called and asked her if she felt she could tell me what the Lord had shown her about me the day we initally met. I did know that it was a positive word, but I didn't know what it was. She told me the Lord had told her two weeks prior to my phone call that I was going to call her. I had never called her to ask for anything for myself. The initial word from the Lord was, "It is through you and through My Spirit that Randy will be given new directions to take. He will witness for Me all over the world, but not until he knows Me better. Soon he will see Me clearer through you."

3. Anointing and prophecy in 1989

During an experience at the Champaign Vineyard, Ron Allen gave a prophetic word: "Wait and see—one day God will raise him up to be a leading evangelist in the Vineyard." This was the most powerful anointing I have ever received. I truly thought I would die if the power became any stronger. I had asked God to confirm whether or not I was called to evangelism.

4. Anointing at Lakeland, January 1994

This was an unusual phenomena, so much so that Rodney Howard-Browne remembered the incident several months later when I met with him, as did his administrator, Karl Strader's son from The Carpenter's Home Church.

While it was occurring, Rodney came to me and said, "This is the fire of God in your hands. Go home and pray for everyone in your church."

I offered to pray the following Sunday, and about 90 percent of the church indicated that they wanted prayer. About 95 percent of those for whom I prayed "fell out" under the Spirit.

5. Prophetic vision by Robyn Mares prior to going to Canada

Robyn, my assistant pastor's wife, saw me riding a wave, a tsunami, from the Southeast United States, cresting over the Midwest, and landing in Southern California, with a Bible and microphone in my hands.

6. Prophetic word from Richard Holcomb (January 19, 1994) before I went to Canada

"Test Me now; test Me now; test Me now. Don't be afraid; I will back you up. I want your eyes to be opened to My resources in the heavens just as Elisha asked for Gehazi's eyes to be opened. And do not be anxious, because when you become anxious, you cannot hear Me."

Richard had been used by God over the past ten years to speak into my life or to help financially without having any contact with me to know of my needs. He always sent the right amount, and his words were always right on. Because of his track record, I placed a lot of stock in his words.

Richard had no idea what was going on in my life when he received this word for me—I was to leave for Canada the next morning.

This word changed my life. For the first time I had a great amount of faith. No longer was I troubled that God would not come when I invited His Spirit to come upon the meetings.

7. Second prophetic word from Richard Holcomb (January 22, 1994) during the first few days of the meetings in Canada

"There are good, better, and best; you are in the best. It is like a professional golfer that breaks through and wins a major tournament. You are taking your ministry to a new level, a new plane. As King David had the mighty men surround him—those who would support him and those he could trust 100 percent—you need these men around you to uplift, support, and pray for you, your ministry, and your family." When Richard gave this word to DeAnne for me, he had heard nothing about what was happening in Toronto.

8. Third prophetic word and action from Richard Holcomb on February 27, 1994, at the Toronto Vineyard

I had contacted Richard to tell him what an impact that initial word had upon my life, to thank him for his faithfulness in giving it, and to invite him to come to Toronto. He came and spent about three days at the meetings.

During one of the meetings God came upon him powerfully. (He said it was the most powerful experience he had ever had.) During this time he received some prophetic words from the Lord. We did not understand at the time most of what was communicated. Some of what he remembers is as follows: "This is the engine, not the caboose, of the train. The power of the engine will come from the fire of the Holy Spirit who is the fuel . . . God will show you the circle you will be in and ministering to—double circles" (Richard kept repeating "double circles" and moved his hands to form two large circles).

"Great power and anointing . . . You will speak to the nations and to people who have different languages. Indian . . . You will not decide when to stop—you will not say you are tired and can go no further . . . Can the clay say to the potter what you will be or to the owner where you will go? When you are tired and cannot hold your arms up by yourself, God will send people under each arm to hold your arms up as He did for Moses."

After this was over, Richard was crying. He said, "I knew you would suffer as Paul did, and I knew this was leading to the cross."

9. Prophetic vision from John Adams of Toronto

He saw me in front of thousands with a Vineyard band behind me. (This was fulfilled at the Benny Hinn crusade in Dallas, Texas, in April 1994.) Right after the vision came to him, he told me that I would one day speak in front of thousands.

10. Prophetic word from Terry and Windy Virgo

The point of this word was that God was going to expand my sphere of influence. He was going to give me apostolic wisdom and was going to open up new spheres of ministry where I would be operating under authority, that I would not have to worry about discerning this when it occurred because it would be so evident and easy to recognize.

They prophesied over me for a long time. Much was said about apostolic wisdom. It was encouraging, but I regret that no one had a tape recorder to record what was said.

11. Prophetic word from Ginny Spratly, early in 1994

God had showed her that I would have an international ministry. "There is a big wave coming, much bigger than the one presently coming; God is preparing you for this big wave which is coming . . . In this last-day ministry (not in it yet), those who move in it have got to be holy unto Him . . . Follow your heart, not another man. Don't run ahead of Him. . . . God is protecting you; you're going to undergo a battle . . . be on guard."

12. David Ruis's prophetic vision in June 1994

"When I look at you, I see Europe over you. I want you to begin praying about going to Europe." I had never traveled outside of North America at that time.

13. Personal prophetic vision

This word came during an angelic visitation to a young seminarian friend of Steve Nicholson's while they were staying in St. Louis for a pastors' conference. There was a lot of prophecy for me, and I remember that he said the angel told him that Kathryn Kuhlman's anointing was going to come on me. Steve believes this young man is the closest person he knows with the level of prophetic anointing that is on Paul Cain.

14. The Bible

Now if you look hard enough it is easy to find a passage which says what you want it to say. This word came to DeAnne when she was distraught over my being away from her while I was in Canada. It came about the end of January or the first week of February. She was asking God what all of this meant. She did not want me to be away from her. She opened her Bible, and, as she looked down at the pages, she felt the Lord had given her Isaiah 49:1–10. She did not understand all of its significance, but she felt sure this was a direct answer from God that brought comfort to her. Later she was telling someone about this experience while she was in Canada. She borrowed the person's Bible to look up Isaiah 49. When she opened the Bible, it fell open right to Isaiah 49.

15. *Prophetic word from Marc Dupont*

I received this word at the summer camp of the Airport Vineyard in August, and it was surprising and helpful to me. One evening John and Carol Arnott, Wes and Stacy Campbell, Marc Dupont, and De Anne and I were together to minister to each other. Marc and Stacy both had prophetic words for me. Part of the prophecy Marc gave me was very surprising. He told me that I would be ministering more outside the Vineyard than inside the Vineyard in the future. (Up until that time I had not ministered outside the Vineyard.)

He also told me that God was getting ready to open doors for me to the Pentecostals, the Assemblies, and the Faith camp. He said he had heard my testimony and knew it would sound bizarre to me, but to "put it on the back burner and wait and see."

I didn't have to wait long; within two weeks I had an invitation to minister at a Faith church. And within a few weeks I had accepted an invitation to minister in one of the largest Faith churches in New Jersey. I don't think I would have been open to accept this invitation had I not received this prophetic word through Marc Dupont.

Even more surprising was what happened at the Catch the Fire conference in October 1994. While there, a distinguished older man from England by the name of David Carr introduced himself. He told me the Holy Spirit had told him to come to this conference. He had enjoyed himself, but he knew there was a purpose for his being at the conference. He had been asking the Holy Spirit why he had been brought to Toronto at the same time I went up to the stage. The Holy Spirit spoke to him when he saw me: "You must talk to that man."

David told me that he was a leader of the largest Pentecostal denomination in England, the Elim Pentecostals. He was a man who had traveled and ministered in twenty-three streams of Pentecostals, Assemblies, and Faith camp churches. He said, "When you get ready to leave America, contact me. I can open the doors to the Pentecostals, the Assemblies, and the Faith camp to you." David actually quoted, almost verbatim, the words

Marc Dupont had prophesied to me only two months earlier.

In addition to these fifteen prophetic words, two imparta-
tions, and the Bible passage quickened to DeAnne, the following
men in leadership have said to me that they see God's call on my
life for what I am doing. These men are not my peers.

Though I do not remember exactly, I do remember that I was
surprised and even somewhat embarrassed by what they said to
me. They were very encouraging words about God's anointing on
my life and how God was going to use me. Each person indicated
that because of what had happened to me during the first two
months of Toronto in 1994, my life would never be the same.

1. Ron Allen—Vineyard regional overseer, part of Indiana and
    Michigan
2. John Arnott—senior pastor of Toronto Airport Christian
    Fellowship
3. Mike Bickle—senior pastor of Metro Vineyard Fellowship
4. Marc Dupont—international itinerant prophetic ministry
5. Steve Nicholson—Vineyard regional overseer, Chicago area
6. Steve Phillips—Vineyard area pastoral coordinator, Midwest
    region
7. Happy Leman—Vineyard regional overseer, Midwest region
8. Fred Wright—Vineyard area pastoral coordinator, Denver area

None of these affirmations was solicited in any manner. They
were spoken to me during the first few months of 1994, soon
after the outbreak of the Spirit at the Airport Vineyard. This was
at a time when I did not recognize the significance of what God
was doing at the Airport Vineyard. It wasn't until the summer of
1994 that we began to realize the significance of those meetings.

One of the most important reasons to believe this renewal is
of God is the fruit that is present. I am not talking about seeds,
but fruit. The testimonies from the meetings have been very
encouraging.

# NOTES

I have two kinds of notes in this section: 1) information about books and magazines forth from which I gathered material, 2) names and personal information about people who were eye-witnesses to healings and other manifestations of God's power. By giving these people's names, I am trying to give readers the opportunity to check out the truthfulness of my claims. Though I was not able to always give a name (due to the personal nature of some events), I verified the accuracy of the testimony to the best of my ability. I hope that the testimonies will help your faith to be released and that I will be considered a trustworthy witness to the acts of Jesus today through the power of the Holy Spirit.

CHAPTER ONE
PASSION

1. Bert and Emmogean Campbell live at the Hamilton Memorial Nursing Home in McLeansboro, Illinois.

2. Reverend Billy Duncan lives in Carmi, Illinois.

CHAPTER THREE
PRESSING IN

1. Tom and Barbara Gooch live in Creal Springs, Illinois.

2. Blaine and Becky Cook live in Tustin, California.

CHAPTER FOUR
PRUNING

1. The identity of the woman who was delivered has been withheld at her request, but the story may be investigated by contacting John Gordon, president of Gordon and Price Engineering, Inc., Marion, Illinois.

2. Mary is not her real name. John Gordon (see note 1) can confirm the events that occurred when we prayed for her.

CHAPTER FIVE
POWER

1. Steve and Jackie Phillips, founder of Equipping Ministries International, live in Rolla, Missouri.

CHAPTER SIX
TORONTO

1. John Wesley, Charles Wesley, and George Whitefield, *Nature of Revival,* ed. and abridged by Claire George Weekley (Minneapolis, MN: Bethany House, 1987).

2. Eifon Evans, *Daniel Rowland and the Great Awakening in Wales* (Edinburgh: Banner of Truth Trust, 1985), 158, as quoted in Guy Chevreau, *Catch the Fire* (Toronto: HarperPerennial, 1994), 209.

3. W.E.C., *This Is That* (Ft. Walsh, PA: Christian Literature Crusade, 1954), 12–15.

4. A. W. Tozer, *The Pursuit of God,* chapter 1.

5. Marc Dupont is on staff at Toronto Airport Christian Fellowship in Toronto, Ontario, Canada.

CHAPTER SEVEN
MOSCOW

1. Nobuo Tanaka pastors Yonezawa Kojo Church in Yonezawa, Yamagata, Japan.

2. For more information about Francis of Assisi, see Kenneth Scott Latourette, *A History of Christianity* (New York: Harper, 1953), 429–433, and Williston Walker, *A History of the Christian Church,* third ed. (New York: Charles Scribner's Sons, 1970) 234–238.

3. For more information about Loyola, see Latourette, 843–848, and Walker, 376–377.

4. Arthur Wallis, *In the Day of Thy Power* (Ft. Walsh, PA: Christian Literature Crusade, 1956), 88.

5. Some information about Zinzendorf came from lectures on church history by Lewis Drummond at the Southern Baptist Theological Seminary in Louisville, Kentucky. For more information about Zinzendorf, see Walker, 450–459.

6. Winkie Pratney, *Revivals* (Lafayette, LA: Huntington House, 1994), 74–76.

SELECT BIBLIOGRAPHY

Arnott, John. *The Father's Blessing.* Orlando, FL: Creation House, 1995.

Bickle, Mike. *Passion for Jesus.* Lake Mary, FL: Creation House, 1993.

———. *Growing in the Prophetic.* Lake Mary, FL: Creation House, 1996.

Blue, Ken. *Authority to Heal.* Downers Grove, IL: InterVarsity Press, 1987.

Campbell, Wesley. *Welcoming a Visitation of the Holy Spirit.* Lake Mary, FL: Creation House, 1995.

Chevreau, Guy. *Pray With Fire: Interceding in the Spirit.* Toronto: Harper Collins Pub., 1995.

———. *Catch the Fire: The Toronto Blessing, An Experience of Renewal and Revival.* London: Marshall Pickering, 1994.

Cooke, Graham. *Developing Your Prophetic Gifting.* Kent, England: Sovereign World Ltd., 1994.

Dawson, John. *Taking Our Cities for God.* Lake Mary, FL: Creation House, 1989.

DeArteaga, William. *Quenching the Spirit.* Lake Mary, FL: Creation House, 1992.

Deere, Jack. *Surprised by the Power of the Spirit.* Grand Rapids, MI: Zondervan Publishing House, 1993.

———. *Surprised by the Voice of God.* Grand Rapids, MI: Zondervan Publishing House, 1996.

Dixon, Patrick. *Signs of Revival.* East Sussex, UK: Kingsway Publications, 1994.

Dupont, Marc. *The Elijah Years* (not available).

Fee, Gordon D. *God's Empowering Presence.* Peabody, MA: Hendrickson Publishers, Inc., 1994.

Foster, Richard J. *Prayer: Finding the Heart's True Home.* San Francisco, CA: HarperSanFrancisco, 1992.

Gott, Ken and Lois. *The Sunderland Refreshing* (not available).

Grieg, Gary S., and Kevin N. Springer, ed. *The Kingdom and the Power.* Ventura, CA: Regal Books, 1993.

Grudem, Wayne. *The Gift of Prophecy in the New Testament Today.* Wheaton, IL: Crossway Books, 1988.

Harper, Michael. *Spiritual Warfare.* Ann Arbor, MI: Servant Publications, 1984.

Helland, Roger. *Let the River Flow: Welcoming Renewal Into Your Church.* South Plainfield, NJ: Bridge-Logos, in press.

Jackson, Bill. *What in the World Is Happening to Us?* Booklet. Toronto: Toronto Airport Christian Fellowship Bookstore.

Jacobs, Cindy. *Possessing the Gates of the Enemy.* Grand Rapids, MI: Chosen Books, 1982.

———. *The Voice of God.* Ventura, CA: Regal Books, 1995.

Kraft, Charles H. *Christianity With Power.* Ann Arbor, MI: Servant Books, 1989.

Lewis, David. *Healing: Fiction, Fantasy or Fact?* London, UK: Hodder and Stoughton, 1989.

Lloyd-Jones, Martyn. *Joy Unspeakable: Power and Renewal in the Holy Spirit.* Wheaton, IL: Harold Shaw Publishers, 1984.

———. *Revival.* Westchester, IL: Crossway Books, 1987.

———. *The Sovereign Spirit.* Wheaton, IL: Harold Shaw Publishers, 1985.

Lovelace, Richard F. *Dynamics of Spiritual Life.* Westmont, IL: InterVarsity Press, 1980.

MacNutt, Francis. *Healing.* New York, NY: Image Books, 1988.

———. *The Power to Heal.* Notre Dame, IN: Ave Maria Press, 1985.

———. *The Prayer That Heals.* Notre Dame, IN: Ave Maria Press, 1981.

———. *Overcome by the Spirit.* Grand Rapids, MI: Chosen Books, 1988.

Mallone, George. *Those Controversial Gifts.* Arlington, TX: Grace Vineyard of Arlington, 1988.

Morphew, Derek. *Renewal Apologetics.* Paper. Toronto: Toronto Airport Christian Fellowship Bookstore.

Nathan, Rich, and Ken Wilson. *Empowered Evangelicals.* Ann Arbor, MI: Servant Publications, 1995.

Payne, Leanne. *Listening Prayer.* Grand Rapids, MI: Baker Books, 1994.

Pickett, Fuschia. *The Next Move of God.* Lake Mary, FL: Creation House, 1994.

Poloma, Margaret. *By Their Fruits: A Sociological Assessment of the Toronto Blessing.* Self-published, 1996.

Pratney, Winkie. *Revival.* Lafayette, LA: Huntington House Publishers, 1994.

Pytches, David. *Prophecy in the Local Church.* London, UK: Hodder and Stoughton, 1993.

———. *Spiritual Gifts in the Local Church.* Minneapolis, MN: Bethany House Publishers, 1988.

Riss, Richard M. *A Survey of 20th-Century Revival Movements in North America.* Peabody, MA: Hendrickson, 1988.

Roberts, David. *The Toronto Blessing.* East Sussex, UK: Kingsway Publications, 1994.

Ryle, James. *A Dream Come True.* Lake Mary, FL: Creation House, 1995.

———. *Hippo in the Garden.* Lake Mary, FL: Creation House, 1993.

Springer, Kevin, ed. *Power Encounters Among Christians in the Western World.* San Francisco, CA: Harper and Row, Publishers, 1988.

White, John. *When the Spirit Comes With Power.* Downers Grove, IL: InterVarsity Press, 1988.

White, Thomas. *The Believer's Guide to Spiritual Warfare.* Ann Arbor, MI: Servant Publications, 1990.

Williams, Don. *Revival: The Real Thing.* La Jolla, CA: Coast Vineyard, 1995.

———. *Signs, Wonders, and the Kingdom of God: A Biblical Guide for the Reluctant Skeptic.* Ann Arbor, MI: Servant Publications, 1989.

Wimber, John. *Power Evangelism.* San Francisco, CA. Harper and Row, Publishers, 1986.

———. *Power Healing.* San Francisco, CA. Harper and Row, Publishers, 1987.

Other Books and Tapes
by Randy Clark

Booklets

God Can Use Little Ol' Me
Prophetic Foundations for Revival
Falling Under the Power of the Holy Spirit
The Baptism of the Holy Spirit
Learning How to Minister Under the Anointing
Cessation or Continuation of Spiritual Gifts?

4-Tape Series
by Randy Clark

Renewal Series
Heal the Sick

2-Tape Series
by Bill and Barbara Cassada

Ten Steps to Freedom
(Deliverance Training)

To order materials or for information about Global Awakening:

Global Awakening
2923 Telegraph Road, St. Louis, MO 63125
Telephone: (314) 416-9239
Fax Number: (314) 416-7051
E-mail: parakletos@ibm.net
Web Site: http://www.globalawakening.com

If you enjoyed reading *Lighting Fires,*
we would like to recommend the following books:

The Father's Blessing
by John Arnott

A wonderful outpouring of the Holy Spirit is happening at John Arnott's church in Toronto, Canada. You've probably heard about it as "The Toronto Blessing." Thankfully, it's not confined to Toronto, and here's your chance to experience it for yourself. With extraordinary first-hand testimonies and sound biblical insight, John Arnott will speak to your heart and show how you can experience a fresh move of the Holy Spirit in your life.

Time to Weep
by Stephen Hill

Inside every man and woman there is a fountain waiting to erupt—a fountain so powerful that it produces its own language . . . the language of tears. *Time to Weep* is God's call for you to weep the tears of repentance, to unleash your own language of tears, and to see the reality of who you are in relation to God.

Available at your local Christian bookstore or from:

Creation House
600 Rinehart Road
Lake Mary, FL 32746

1-800-283-4561, fax
Web site: http://www.creationhouse.com

Yes! The same people who bring you Charisma magazine each month now offer you an entire warehouse of Spirit-led books! Call now to receive your FREE copy of the CBW Resource Catalog and receive 20 percent off the retail price of every title you select.

Charisma Book Warehouse is your best source for powerful, Spirit-led books by great teachers like T.D. Jakes, Joyce Meyers, John Bevere, Mike Bickle, Cathy Lechner, and many more!

The Charisma Book Warehouse is not a "club" that you have to join. There is absolutely no obligation to buy at any time. Simply call *1-800-599-5750* and start getting your favorite Spirit-led books directly through the mail for 20 percent off!

For more information on how to receive your FREE CBW Resource Catalog call

1-800-599-5750

or mail your name and address to:

CBW

P.O. Box 520670
Longwood, FL 32752-0670

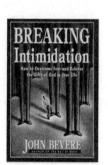
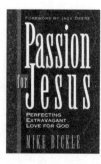